Plantology

Plantology

30 ACTIVITIES AND OBSERVATIONS FOR EXPLORING THE WORLD OF PLANTS

Michael Elsohn Ross

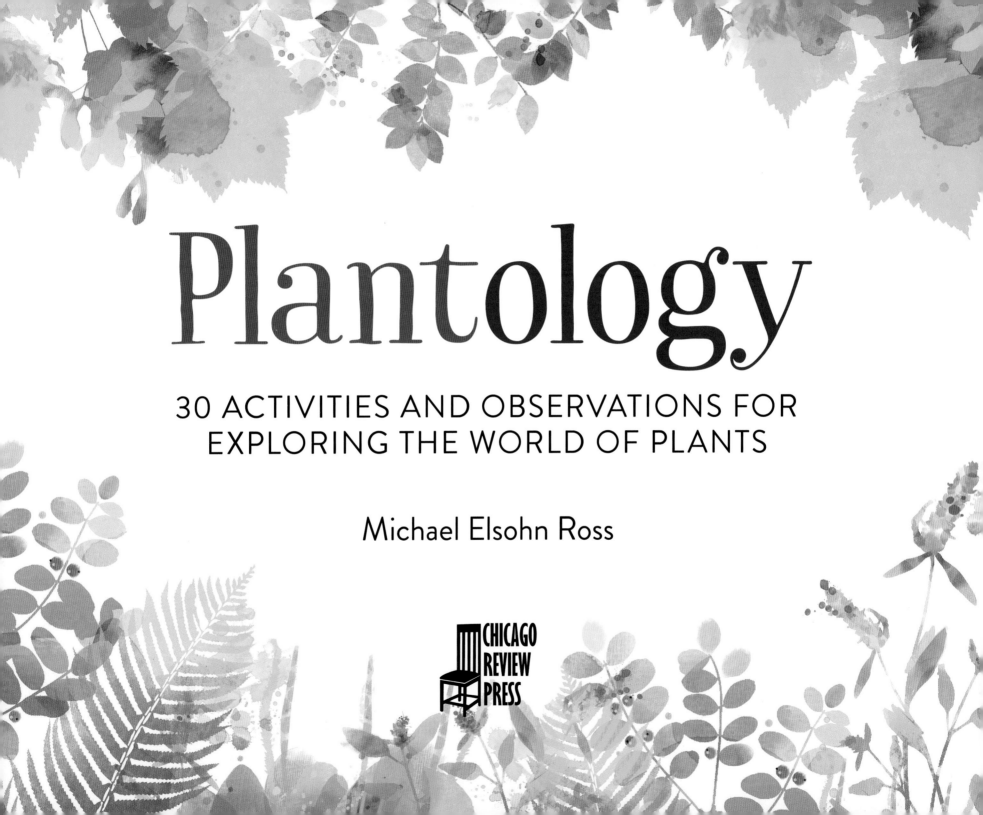

CHICAGO REVIEW PRESS

Copyright © 2019 by Michael Elsohn Ross
Published by Chicago Review Press Incorporated
814 North Franklin Street
Chicago, Illinois 60610
ISBN 978-1-61373-737-8

Library of Congress Cataloging-in-Publication Data
Names: Ross, Michael Elsohn, 1952– author.
Title: Plantology : 30 activities and observations for exploring the world of
  plants / Michael Elsohn Ross.
Description: Chicago, Illinois : Chicago Review Press Incorporated, [2019] |
  Audience: Age 7+ | Includes bibliographical references and index.
Identifiers: LCCN 2018028752 (print) | LCCN 2018029606 (ebook) | ISBN
  9781613737385 (adobe pdf) | ISBN 9781613737408 (epub) | ISBN
9781613737392
  (kindle) | ISBN 9781613737378 (paperback)
Subjects: LCSH: Plants—Juvenile literature.
Classification: LCC QK49 (ebook) | LCC QK49 .R67 2019 (print) | DDC 581—
dc23 LC record available at https://lccn.loc.gov/2018028752

Cover and interior design: Sarah Olson
Cover photos: FRONT: pond lily, cardinal flowers, coleus, bee fly, redshank
  moss, and iris seeds from Wikimedia Commons; butterfly, kiwi, and root
  from Shutterstock.com. BACK: vine, butterfly, and flower from 123rf.com.
Interior illustrations: Lindsey Cleworth Schauer, pp. 5, 58, and 61; all other
  illustrations by Michael Elsohn Ross
Interior photos: Wikimedia Commons unless otherwise indicated

Printed in the United States of America
5 4 3 2 1

This book is dedicated to my grandnieces, Eloise and Georgia; my grandnephew, Levi; my granddaughter, Genesis; and other young people around the world who are the future caretakers of our plant friends.

Contents

Acknowledgments

I thank two mentors, Bob Fry and Carl Sharsmith, who are no longer living but continue to inspire me to investigate the plant life of the Sierra Nevada. I'm grateful to Professor Everett Schlinger, who opened my eyes to insect-plant relationships, especially pollination, and Professors Joe McBride and Ed Stone, who rekindled my connection to plants. Most importantly, thank you, Davy, for teaching me about plants when we were kids in the woods.

Introduction

One of my earliest memories is of a secret place inside a shady enclosure of vines at my home when I was three years old. Later, I lived in another town, in a newly built neighborhood bordered by woods that I explored with my friends. It was here that I truly entered the realm of plants. I encountered thorny briars, thick grapevines, velvet moss carpets, wild garlic, and stately rhododendron groves. I felt at home in this world. Without being aware of it, I had become a plant person.

By the time I was 10 years old, this wooded wonderland was transformed into more streets and houses. This great loss both saddened and angered me. How could people do this?

In college I studied botany, and when I was 22 years old I got a job at Yosemite National Park in the Sierra Nevada mountains of California, a land rich with an amazing variety of plants and people to learn from. Living here for over 40 years now and teaching people about Yosemite has been a continuous learning experience. There are always new questions, mysteries, and things to notice that I was unaware of before.

I hope this book encourages you, too, to notice and learn about the plants you see around you every day or when you travel to a new place. Maybe you will simply come to appreciate them in a new way, or even begin your own life journey into wilderness study.

Happy reading and exploring!

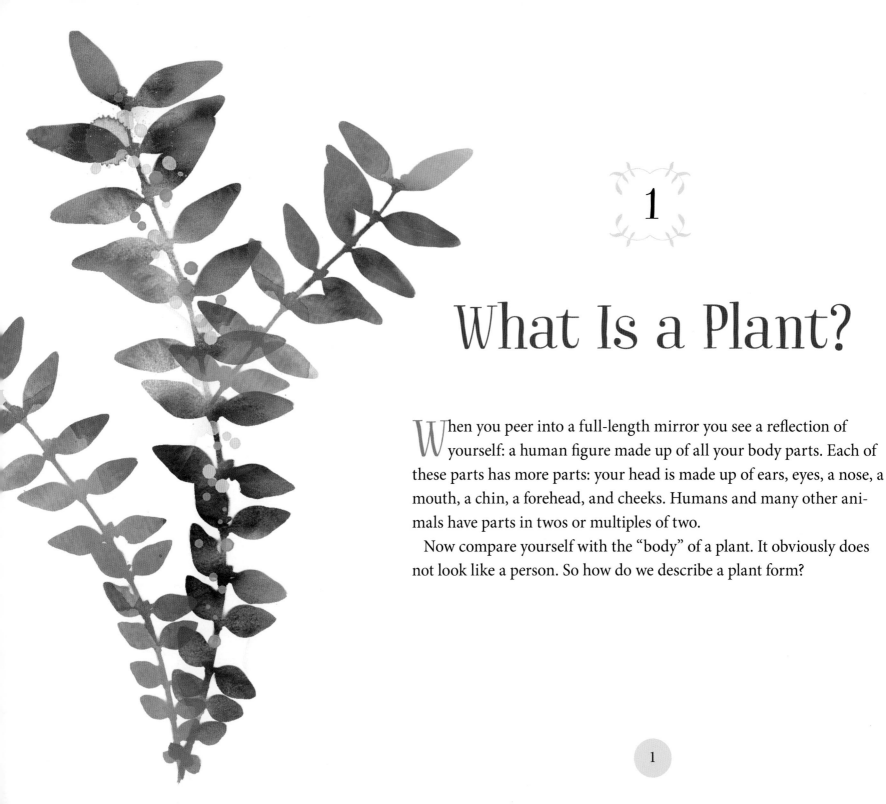

1

What Is a Plant?

When you peer into a full-length mirror you see a reflection of yourself: a human figure made up of all your body parts. Each of these parts has more parts: your head is made up of ears, eyes, a nose, a mouth, a chin, a forehead, and cheeks. Humans and many other animals have parts in twos or multiples of two.

Now compare yourself with the "body" of a plant. It obviously does not look like a person. So how do we describe a plant form?

Let's use a buttercup as an example. The buttercup plant is anchored by roots, out of which grows a stem. From the stem grow other stems, each bearing leaves, **buds**, and flowers. Each of these parts has more parts, just as a human arm has a hand with fingers and fingernails.

Look for buttercups growing in lawns and parks.

PLANT JOURNAL

Scrutinize, scribble, sketch! A plant journal can be like a travelogue describing the plants you meet. Make a journal and use it to record observations and sketches on your own or as you work through the activities in this book.

MATERIALS

- Notebook with unlined pages
- Colored markers, or scissors and old seed catalogs or gardening magazines (to decorate cover)
- Glue
- Your sharp eyes
- Magnifying glass
- Pen or pencil
- Colored pencils

1. Decorate the cover of your journal with drawings or with pictures cut out from seed catalogs or garden magazines.

2. Take an expedition around your neighborhood, school, or anywhere else you are likely to see plants.

3. Choose a plant to observe closely. Use your magnifying glass to get a close-up view.

4. Write down words that describe the unique characteristics of the plant.

5. Make sketches of different parts, such as leaves, stems, or flowers.

6. Record the location of the plant and any questions you have.

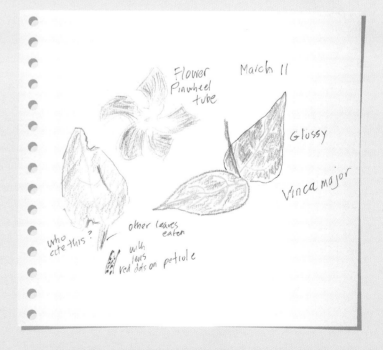

2

PLANT PORTRAIT

Observe, compose, sketch! Create a portrait of a houseplant or an outdoor plant in your yard or neighborhood.

MATERIALS

- 🗡 Your sharp eyes
- 🗡 Magnifying glass
- 🗡 Plant journal
- 🗡 Pencil
- 🗡 Crayons, colored pencils, or markers

1. Choose an indoor or outdoor plant to observe.

2. Examine the plant carefully with the magnifying glass. Take notice of the shape of the stem, leaves, and other parts.

3. In your plant journal, do a quick sketch of the whole plant in pencil before adding details in color.

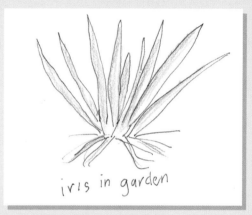

Sample sketch of an iris plant.

Plant or Not?

Do all plants have leaves, roots, stems, flowers, and seeds? No. Unlike birds, which all have feathers, not all plants possess the same features. For example, Indian pipe lacks leaves. Watermeal, a common pond plant, is missing stems and roots. Mosses have leaves and stems but no flowers, seeds, or real roots. They have rootlike structures that anchor them but don't transport water.

The plant kingdom contains a wide range of **organisms**, including green algae, mosses, ferns, herbs, vines, shrubs, and trees (which are not covered in this book). The majority of plants use sunlight to produce their own food from nutrients and water, though there are exceptions like Indian pipe, which doesn't need leaves because it gets sugars from soil fungi.

Plant Speak

People who study plants are called botanists. Like artists, electricians, and nurses, they use a special vocabulary. Botanical

Indian pipe.

3

language allows botanists to describe plants in a concise way. The only problem is if you don't know the language, you have no idea what a botanist means when he or she says that a plant is an autotroph (makes its own food) or is **biennial** (lives its whole life in two years).

Learning a new language can be a challenge, but just imagine being able to

The French named this plant *dent de lion*, meaning "tooth of the lion," because of its tooth-edged leaves. Mispronounced and misspelled by the English, it became *dandelion*. *Shutterstock*

speak like a botanist with words like *pistil*, *glochid*, and *gymnosperm* rolling off your tongue. The next paragraph includes a few new words to start with.

Plants belong to the kingdom Plantae. Each unique type of plant is classed as a **species**. The common dandelion species, for example, is *Taraxacum officinale*. This name is composed of two parts: *Taraxacum* is the **genus** name, and *officinale* is the species name. There are 60 other species of *Taraxacum* growing around the world. One species in California is very rare, one in Japan has white flowers, and another in Kazakhstan produces a natural rubber.

The First Plants: Algae

The first plants to appear on Earth were algae, which show up in fossils that date back 500 million years. Some algae were simply a single cell that used sunlight to transform a gas called carbon dioxide and water into sugars through a process called **photosynthesis**. Others were minute threadlike strands, or filaments, that floated in water. They were very basic plants that lacked leaves, roots, flowers, and seeds.

Among algae living on Earth today are micro (small) and macro (large) species. In freshwater ponds, a green micro alga called

spirogyra can be found growing in large, slimy masses. Chlorella is another single-cell alga known for its rapid reproduction.

Along the seashore, you may find a common green macro alga, such as sea lettuce or gutweed, growing in shallow water or washed up on the shore. Dwarf rockweed, another macro alga, can be found clinging to rocks submerged during high tide. These marine algae, or seaweeds, take in water and nutrients from seawater through all of their tissues. Unlike most land plants, they don't have roots or interior **veins** to transport water or nutrients.

Solar Food Factories: Photosynthesis

Every day as sunlight shines upon leaves, something amazing occurs. We can't see, feel, or hear it, but we can see the results as we watch plants grow. Using the energy from sunlight, plants transform water and carbon dioxide into sugar and oxygen in a process called photosynthesis.

This action depends on a substance called chlorophyll, which breaks apart molecules of water and carbon dioxide and re-forms them as sugar and oxygen. Chlorophyll is found in plant structures called chloroplasts, which are like food factories

ALGAE EXPEDITION

Seek, search, but *don't* touch! You can look for algae in saltwater or fresh water. For safety reasons, invite an adult to join you while visiting any bodies of water to conduct your search. Freshwater algae may grow in large masses in ponds, canals, and lakes, especially where these bodies of water have been polluted. Runoff from farms and factories may contain fertilizers, manure, or other waste that certain types of alga thrive in. These thick masses of alga that turn bodies of water into green soups or slimy mats are called algal blooms. **Warning:** Do not touch these algae! Just observe.

If you live near or can visit the seashore, go during low tide to view the greatest variety of algae.

Excess nutrients cause algal blooms.

where sugars are constantly being produced. These sugars are food for both the plant and any animals that eat the plant.

Plants and animals need to take in oxygen to release the energy from the sugars. This process, called **respiration**, creates carbon dioxide that is released into the air. Plants respire at night, while animals respire both day and night.

In extreme hot or cold temperatures, plants photosynthesize more slowly or not at all. Plants growing in the chilly far north have leaves especially adapted for absorbing heat and light from the sun. These plants

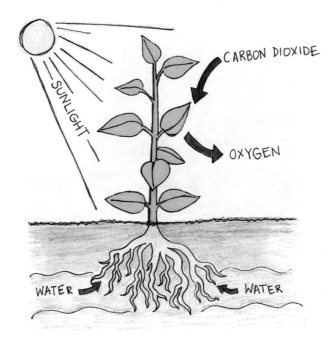

SUNLIGHT

CARBON DIOXIDE

OXYGEN

WATER

WATER

CELLS AND MORE CELLS

Cells are the building blocks of all organisms. They are composed of a cell membrane, a kind of skin, that holds a material called cytoplasm, which contains proteins and nucleic acids. The largest plant cell is a single-cell alga called *Acetabularia*. It looks like an underwater mushroom and can grow as high as a tennis ball.

Scientists believe the first life forms to appear on Earth, about three billion years ago, were single-cell organisms called Archaea. These microscopic cells were the only organisms for a long time before multicellular life evolved.

Depending on their size, most plants contain billions of cells. A human is made up of more than 10 trillion cells!

Plant cell diagram.

nucleus

cell membrane

cell wall

chloroplast

Plant Cell

often grow low to the ground to benefit from the warmth of sun-heated soils and to avoid cold winds.

Plants in dry, hot deserts survive because they have leaves that conserve water. Desert plants also have hairs that shade the leaf surface and reflect sunlight, which helps them stay cool.

The hundreds of thousands of plant species have an incredible variety of leaf shapes and sizes. Different types of leaves enable each plant to photosynthesize for each special growing condition.

Humble Mosses

Growing in sidewalk cracks, on shaded tree trunks, and on roof shingles, mosses usually don't earn the oohs and aahs reserved for flashy flowers and colorful vines. But

Sphagnum moss was used to treat wounds because of its antibacterial properties.

they do deserve respect for being the first plants to colonize the Earth's land surface more than 450 million years ago.

Without true roots to suck up water or stems to stand tall, mosses still thrive. Using water from moist soil, rain, and fog, they grow where bigger, showier plants can't survive. Red roof moss is one of the first plants to appear after a fire. Antarctic moss withstands frigid weather by growing on penguin poop. Though small and seemingly fragile, Antarctic moss buried in frozen ground for more than 1,000 years can be revived to grow again. Sphagnum, also called peat moss, can increase in weight more than 25 times when it gets wet. It's no wonder that it was used as the original disposable diaper. Not only did it soak up baby pee, but the moss's natural acidity also prevented diaper rash.

Scientists believe that mosses may have even changed the Earth's climate from hot to cold by removing carbon dioxide from the Earth's atmosphere. Carbon dioxide acts as a blanket that holds in the Earth's heat. As mosses grow they release acids that dissolve the surface of rocks. During this process, carbon dioxide gas is removed from the air and combined with water to become carbonic acid. In this form, carbon is carried to the sea by streams and rivers,

 **TRY THIS!**

VISIT THE MOSS WORLD

Peer, poke, pet! When moss is moist, it is a soft and intricate green landscape teeming with tiny creatures.

MATERIALS

- Your sharp eyes
- Magnifying glass
- Pen or pencil
- Plant journal

1. Look for moss outside. You might find moss in shady locations at the base of a tree or on its trunk, in a sidewalk crack, or on a forest floor. Notice the shape of the moss's stems and leaves. Using a magnifying glass, you might see a tiny forest of fernlike plants. You might also see a landscape of strange forms, from tonguelike leaves to tiny spears, and even structures that look like tiny palm trees and vases. Liverworts, hornworts, and mosses are known as bryophytes, from the Greek meaning "tree-moss plant."

2. Look for creatures living in the moss, such as mites or springtails. Mites eat both plant material and other small creatures. Springtails devour **spores**, pollen, bacteria, and strands of fungi. Both are arthropods—animals with jointed legs. Like insects, springtails have six legs, while mites have eight legs like their close relatives, spiders.

3. Record your observations in your plant journal.

where it is locked away in carbonate rocks, such as limestone. Millions of years ago, when mosses were the dominant land plant, a massive amount of carbon was removed from the air in this way and transformed into rock.

As more and more carbon was captured in the sea and stored in rock, the blanket of carbon dioxide covering Earth became thinner and held in less of the Earth's heat. The planet cooled, and an ice age began.

For the next 100 million years mosses and their relatives, liverworts and hornworts, were the main plants growing on land. Because they have no roots, they grew only in wet or moist areas.

Moss Cousins

The name of the moss relative liverwort comes from the liver-like shape of the plant's thallus (leaflike structure). Over 100 years ago, people believed a plant or plant part shaped like an organ in the human body could be used as a medicine to cure ailments of that organ. **Wort** is a very old word for a plant with a medicinal use.

Liverwort is still used in China to treat liver disorders such as jaundice and hepatitis.

Another moss cousin, hornwort, is named for the hornlike shape of its reproductive structure. Unlike mosses, hornworts and liverworts have flattened leaflike structures. Mosses' reproductive structures look like caps on stalks. Liverworts' structures look like small umbrellas, and hornworts' structures resemble animal horns.

Plants with Plumbing

Picture a forest, not of pine and oak trees but of giant plants with trunks bearing rings of feathery branches. You might spy

giant amphibians or insects roaming the swampy forest floor. Huge dragonflies with wingspans of three feet (75 centimeters) dart through the air. This world has been revealed by fossils of plants and animals discovered in 350-million-year-old coal deposits. These ancient plants existed long before the days of dinosaurs. Unlike mosses, these plants, called lycopods, had leaves, each with a single vein. With this simple plumbing system, water could flow up into the plants' stems and leaves. These plants could grow taller than the ground-hugging mosses, liverworts, and hornworts. In fact, one species, *Lepidodendron* (meaning "scale tree"), grew up to 100 feet (30 meters) tall.

Liverworts are related to mosses.

An artist imagined this scene of an ancient lycopod forest.

Just like the modern descendants of ancient dragonflies with three-foot (1-meter) wingspans, the modern relatives of these early forest plants have also shrunk in size. Modern lycopods, such as spike moss, club moss, and quillworts, are all low-growing plants. Both spike mosses and club mosses have scalelike leaves, short branching stems, and simple roots. One species of spike moss is called resurrection moss. In arid areas, during long periods without rain, it curls inward as it dries up. Later, when it receives water, the leaves suddenly unfold and turn green.

Many of the club mosses, such as ground pine that grows on the forest floor, look like miniature trees. Named for their hollow, quill-like leaves that can grow up to three feet (about 1 meter) long, quillworts grow in wet or moist places. Some species live underwater.

Feathery Ferns and Hairy Horsetails

Three hundred million years ago, ferns became so dominant that this period is known as the Age of Ferns. The feather-like leaves of ferns, called fronds, are found in coal deposits along with a closely related plant called horsetail. Once treelike, most species of ferns and horsetails are now low-growing. Horsetails are also called scouring brushes because their tough leaves are useful for cleaning pots.

Ferns grow throughout the world, from the small brittle fern growing on islands in the Arctic to the bog fern found only on Tristan da Cunha, a remote island in the South Atlantic Ocean. Ferns and horsetails have a more complex vein, or **vascular**, structure than the plants that came before them.

Unlike a rose bush or bean plant, ferns grow from rootlike stems called **rhizomes** that lie on the ground. From these stems grow upright, stemlike structures called stipes. The upper part of the stipe, where leaflike pinnae (leaflets) grow, is called the rachis (meaning "spine"). The stipe, rachis, and pinna are all parts of the fern frond.

The underside of pinnae may have small round or oval structures. Called sori, these are clusters of sporangia, which produce spores. New ferns grow from spores.

(*top*) A fern grows from a rhizome.

(*right*) The rust-colored structures on the underside of this fern leaf are called sori.

Advanced Plumbing

Plants that have roots and well-developed plumbing to transport water and sugars are called vascular plants. They grow in a variety of forms.

- **Forbs:** A dandelion weed, a broccoli plant, and a sunflower all have non-woody stems and are called forbs or herbaceous plants. Forbs can be as tiny as duckweed or as large as a banana plant, which grows to the size of a small tree but lacks a woody trunk.

- **Shrubs:** A plant with many woody stems, like a rose or blueberry plant, is called a shrub or bush. Some shrubs, like alpine laurels, may grow only a few inches high, while others like redbud may grow 20 feet (6 meters) tall. Shrubs usually have well-developed root systems and stems.

- **Vines:** Plants like honeysuckle or poison ivy that sprawl along the ground like a snake or climb up tree trunks or other surfaces are called vines. Vines have flexible stems that may become rigid as they age. Some are herbaceous, such as morning glory, and others are woody, such as wisteria.

  Vines climb and cling. Aerial roots on ivy plants allow them to attach to tree trunks, rocks, or building surfaces as they grow upward and outward. Grapevines attach with tendrils, and morning glory vines twine around trees or trellises. As climbing roses grow upward, their thorns grip and hold the plant in place.

A potato plant, like many garden crops, is a forb.

Plant Planet

Photos taken of the earth from satellites show the green of plants. Most of Earth's land surface is clothed in vegetation, whether vast grasslands or forest, agricultural fields or shrubs. In tropical zones vegetation appears lush, while in desert regions it is sparse. Across the planet, plants have adapted to the earth's different climates and soils.

Desert plants such as cacti are able to grow by storing water. Plants on the highest mountains hug the ground to take advantage of the sun-warmed soils and rock. Plants in wet, tropical rain forests have drip tips on the ends of their leaves that shed water to prevent molds from growing on leaf surfaces.

All animals depend on plants. Many dine on plant parts. Caterpillars and cows graze on leaves. Pandas and porcupines munch stems and trunks. Cicadas and moles dine on roots. Finches and weevils devour seeds. Earthworms and houseflies digest dead plants. Other animals depend on eating these plant-eaters. Robins breakfast on earthworms. Mountain lions lunch on deer.

Without plants, there would be no animals. Most plants produce their own food, whereas animals, including humans, depend on food from plants or from animals that eat plants. So, make sure to thank the plants on your plate the next time you eat.

2

Sprout and Get a Grip

Floating in the breeze, latching onto your sock, sprinkled on your sandwich bun, wedged between your teeth—seeds are promises of new lives and future generations of plants.

Each seed embryo holds genetic instructions for how the embryo will grow into a mature plant and continue the existence of its species. Like a space capsule sent on a mission to another planet, a seed has the right equipment and materials to establish a successful colony.

Diagram of a bean seed.

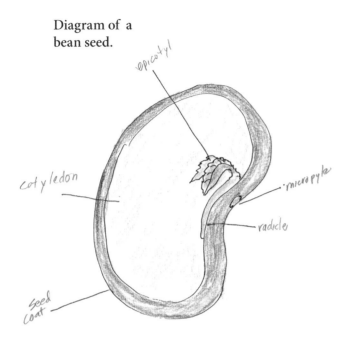

Corn is a grass and has only one seed leaf (left). Squash is a dicotyledon and therefore has two seed leaves (right). *Shutterstock (left)*

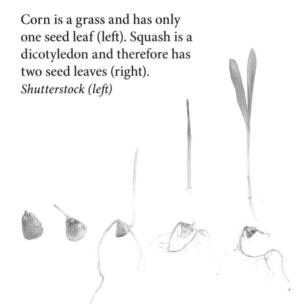

Seeds of Life

Within each seed is a cotyledon, the very first leaf or pair of leaves. Flowering plants are split into two main groups: the mono-cotyledons (*mono-* means "one"), such as grasses and lilies, which have one seed leaf, and the dicotyledons (*di-* means "two"), such as dandelions and radishes, which have two seed leaves.

Both monocotyledon and dicotyledon embryos have a first root, called a **radicle**, that develops into the seedling's root. The embryo gets its initial energy to sprout into a seedling from food stored in a part called the endosperm, or from food stored in the cotyledons.

The Language of Seeds

In English and other languages, certain sayings refer to seeds. An old, worn-out item of clothing may be called *seedy*. A partial idea may be called a *kernel* of an idea. Money used to start a project may be called *seed money*. In botany, there is a special language to describe seeds. Seed shapes may be described using the following terms.

🌿 **Discoid:** Platelike or disklike, such as green amaranth or quinoa seeds.

🌿 **Lenticular:** Lens-shaped, such as lentil seeds.

🌿 **Obconic:** Shaped like an upside-down cone, such as sneezeweed seeds.

Mustard seeds are only 1 to 2 millimeters (0.04–0.08 inches) in diameter.

- **Ovate:** Egg-shaped, such as pumpkin seeds.
- **Spheric:** Shaped like a miniature globe, such as mustard seeds.
- **Triangular:** Shaped like mini pyramids, such as buckwheat groats seeds.

Traveling Seeds

A seed is like a magic suitcase containing all that is needed to create a new plant. Each plant has special needs for growth. These needs include the right amount of sunlight, the best type of soil, and water.

Some seeds simply fall from the parent plant, but other seeds travel to new locations. Dandelion or milkweed seeds, with their feathery parachutes, easily drift off in the breeze to a new spot. The seeds of lupines are ejected as the pod dries and twists. When an animal eats a raspberry, the fruit is broken down but the seeds pass through the animal's digestive system, where digestive enzymes thin the seed coats, making it possible for the seeds to germinate (begin to grow) when they are deposited in the animal's droppings.

The seeds of storksbill and stickseed hitchhike on the fur of passing animals and lodge wherever they are shed. Seeds in

START A SEED COLLECTION

Search, collect, sort! Go on a seed hunt and discover seeds in your kitchen, inside fruits, and outdoors in lawns and gardens.

MATERIALS

- 🐦 Quart-sized resealable plastic bag
- 🐦 Clear adhesive tape
- 🐦 Stiff paper cut in 3-inch (8-centimeter) squares
- 🐦 Pen or pencil
- 🐦 Sheet of newspaper
- 🐦 Plant journal

1. Look for seeds in your kitchen. (Be sure to get permission from an adult, and put containers back where you found them.) The spice rack is a good place to check. Save seeds from tomatoes or cucumbers that you eat. Scrape the seeds off buns, rolls, or bagels. Store the seeds in a plastic bag. When you're done searching, tape one of each kind of seed on a paper square and label it with the name of the seed.

2. Search for seeds outdoors in a garden, field, woods, or weed patch. You can find them by collecting pods or shaking withered flowers over a sheet of newspaper. As in step 1, tape one of each type of seed to a paper square and label it with the name (or, if you don't know the name, a description) of the plant.

3. After you have finished collecting, display the cards and sort them into groups based on whatever characteristics you choose (size, color, shape).

4. Record your observations in a plant journal.

5. You can set aside a few of each kind of seed, except for ones from baked goods, for a later activity.

dandelion

NAKED OR CLOTHED?

Like people, seeds can be naked or clothed.

The majority of shrub and herb species belong to a group called angiosperms (from the Latin words *angio*, meaning "covered," and *sperma*, meaning "seed"). Angiosperms, also known as flowering plants, have "clothed seeds"—seeds protected by a **seed coat**.

A group of plants called gymnosperms (from the Latin words *gymno*, meaning "naked," and *sperma*, meaning "seed") have "naked seeds"—seeds without seed coats. These are the first type of seeds that appeared on the planet. Most of the plants in this naked seed group are trees, especially trees with cones, such as pines, firs, and cedars.

bodies of water like ponds, such as those of water lilies, float away from the parent plant and then sink to the bottom, where they take root. Mangrove seeds, protected in their seed pods, may embark on a long sea voyage to far-off shores.

Some seeds, such as those of violets and wake-robins, feature a fleshy package of oils and proteins that attract ants. Worker ants haul these special seeds, called elaiosomes, back to the colony, where the ant larvae devour the tasty packets. The remaining seed is removed to the colony's waste disposal site, where it is deposited in a pile of ant droppings, dead and decaying insect bodies, and other decomposing plant parts that are rich in fertilizers and nutrients.

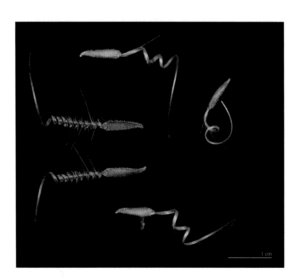

Storksbill seeds hitchhike on passing animals.

Thus the seed ends up in a great place to sprout, far away from its parent plant. Scientists call this transportation process myrmecochory, which means "ant dispersal" in Greek (*myrmex* = ant, *kore* = dispersal).

The Right Date to Germinate

After a seed ends up on the ground it will remain there, protected from rain and snow, heat and cold, by its tough shell. Each seed needs to sprout at a time when temperatures are best for growth.

Geranium, monkshood, and other plants growing in a location with cold winters may have to go through a period of cold before the seed will sprout. Some seeds require special conditions to sprout. In regions where plants experience periodic wildfires, certain species are especially adapted to germinating after a burn. Seeds of fire poppies and other plants that require fires to create the conditions they need to grow may lie dormant, at rest, for 80 years between fires. During a fire, germination is triggered by cues such as smoke, high temperatures, nutrients from burned vegetation, or more groundwater. In spring, flowers, such as fire poppies, appear in great numbers on a burned area following a fire.

Seeds of some desert plants may stay dormant for long periods and are protected from damage from heat and drought, periods without rain, until germinated by heavy rains. During these rains, the seed coats are worn down as the seeds roll along in surface water. The seeds of fruits must have their seed coats worn away by digestive acids. The seeds of mistletoe berries may end up on a tree limb after passing through a bird's digestive system or be shed onto a branch after sticking to a bird's foot.

Tiny Seed Meets Tiny Spore

Orchids have not only the largest number of species but also the smallest seeds. One million orchid seeds can fit in a seed capsule only a few inches long. Orchid seeds lack food reserves, which most seeds have. Therefore, since they contain only an embryo, they can be quite tiny. After being infected by a fungus, which provides it with sugar and nutrients, the embryo transforms into a small ball called a protocorm. Without fungus, the seed would never be able to germinate and become a seedling.

Soon the protocorm turns green, and after a while it sprouts its first leaf and roots. As the seedling grows and produces

HEY, SPROUT!

Moisten, wait, watch, and record! Discover what a sprout is all about. Are all sprouts the same? When seeds germinate or sprout, they have a radicle and cotyledons (first leaves).

MATERIALS

- Paper towels
- 2 same-sized pie tins
- A variety of seeds (use some of those you collected plus brown rice grains)
- Measuring cup
- Water
- Pen or pencil
- Plant journal

1. Put a couple of paper towels on a pie tin.

2. Place the seeds on top of the paper towels.

3. Lay two paper towels over the seeds and pour ¼ cup of water onto the towels. Cover with the other pie tin. Store in a secure location.

4. Check on the seeds each day. As needed, add small amounts (a teaspoon at a time) of water to keep the towels moist.

5. After three days, check to see if any seeds have sprouted. Make a sketch in your plant journal of one or more seeds as they sprout. How many seed leaves does each sprout have?

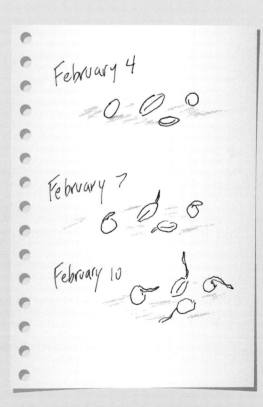

RELIABLE WHEN VIABLE

Some seeds, such as those from some willow species, must sprout within a couple of months of landing on the ground. If they don't, they lose the ability to germinate. The seeds of other shrubs, like wild lilac, which grows in areas with periodic wildfires, remain dormant between fires. These dormant periods can last decades. Seeds of garden plants vary in how long they can remain viable (able to sprout). After a year, parsley seeds are rarely able to sprout, while beet seeds remain viable for four years or more.

its own sugar through photosynthesis, it no longer needs the help of the fungus.

Seed Eaters

Seeds are rich in concentrated nutrients provided for the embryo as it sprouts. Many animals depend on seeds for food. They gulp them, crunch and munch them, and even scoop out the insides.

- **Cozy cradles:** Weevils are beetles that have a snoutlike mouth with jaws at the tip. A female maize weevil chews through the seed coat, nibbles a bit of the insides, and lays a tiny oval egg inside the seed before covering the hole with a waxy plug. Over her life, which lasts less than one year, she can lay eggs in 300 to 400 seeds. In the cozy, safe interior of the seed, a grub devours every bit of food and transforms into a pupa. When it becomes an adult, it chews an exit hole in the shell and seeks a mate. All that remains is a hollow seed coat littered with weevil frass (poop). The maize weevil lays eggs not only in corn kernels but also in oat, barley, and rice grains, as well as pea and buckwheat seeds. Farmers consider this weevil a pest. Bike riders, however, appreciate puncture vine weevils for their work in destroying puncture vine seeds, which can pop bike tires.

Seed- and stem-eating weevils have been used to get rid of this unpopular plant.

- **Mexican jumping bean:** When the little caterpillar that lives in this seed arches one direction, then the other, the seed bounces and moves. With luck it reaches shade, where it's cooler. To anyone watching, it's a mystery how the seed can jump. In Mexico, where the caterpillars live, people call the seeds *frijoles* (beans) *saltarines* (jumping). That is how these seeds got the name *Mexican jumping beans*. North of the Mexican border, they are sold as a novelty. However, the seed is not actually a bean. It comes from a plant in the spurge family, the same family poinsettias belong to. After months inside the seed, the caterpillar emerges as a moth and mates. If it is a female, she lays her eggs in another seed.

- **Bobwhite appetite:** At the beginning of the 20th century, young Margaret Morse studied the feeding habits of a wild chicken-like bird called a bobwhite. Named for their call that sounds like "Bob White, Bob White," these birds were in danger of being hunted to extinction like the passenger pigeon,

SURPRISE GARDEN

Dig, water, watch! Soil is full of seeds, many of them too small to notice. In a newly tilled garden bed planted with garden seeds, seeds of other plants may also sprout. Plants that grow where we don't want them to grow are called weeds. For example, the California poppy, the state flower of California, is considered a weed in Europe. Everlasting pea, a weed in California, is native to Europe, where it is prized in gardens. Cultivate a patch of soil and you might be surprised at what grows there.

MATERIALS

- Spade or shovel
- Rake
- Water
- Pen or pencil
- Plant journal
- Camera (optional)

1. In spring or summer, get an adult's permission to dig up and rake a plot (about 3 feet by 3 feet [1 meter by 1 meter]) of garden.

2. Water the plot with a watering can or hose with the nozzle set on spray.

3. Check the plot every few days.

4. When small seedlings appear, sketch them in your plant journal. You may also want to photograph them.

5. Once they begin to flower, you might be able to identify them in a plant identification guide for your region.

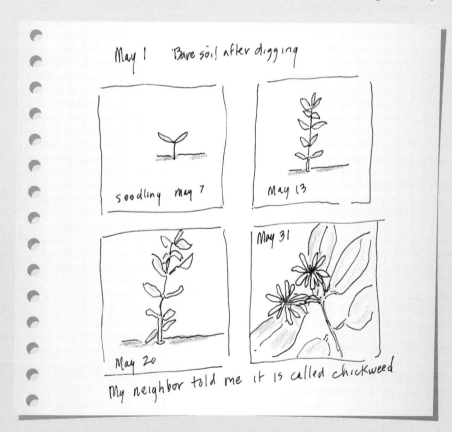

May 1   Bare soil after digging

seedling   may 7

May 13

May 20

May 31

My neighbor told me it is called chickweed

These seedlings sprouted from bare soil.

which became extinct in 1914. Hoping her research would verify the bobwhite's importance in controlling insects and weed populations, Margaret carefully recorded how many bugs and weed seeds the birds ate each day. At the end of her study, she estimated that a single bobwhite might consume 75,000 insects and 5 million weed seeds in a single summer.

🍃 **Doves, finches, sparrows, chickadees, jays, titmice, cardinals, and grosbeaks:** These are among the many groups of birds that consume large numbers of seeds. Finches and cardinals have thick bills used to crack seeds. A cardinal's seed-cracking bill is much bigger than a chickadee's. Small rodents such as mice, chipmunks, and kangaroo rats also depend on seeds for much of their diet.

Plants Without Seeds

The first plants to appear on Earth were alga filaments, or threads, that lived in water and did not need leaves, roots, flowers, or seeds. Plant eggs and sperm floated in the water and ran into each other; they fused and formed a new plant. Mosses became the first plant to survive on land, by developing stems, rootlike growths called rhizoids, and a two-part reproductive system.

In the first stage of reproduction, moss sperm swim through the water to a wine bottle–shaped structure that holds the eggs. After an egg is fertilized, it transforms into a threadlike tower. Its bulbous top has many spores that eventually drift away in the breeze. Spores that land in a moist location will become a new patch of moss. Other land plants—hornworts, liverworts, horsetails, quillworts, and ferns—also produce spores instead of seeds.

SEED STATS

>>>

Here are some fascinating facts about the biggest, smallest, and other remarkable seeds.

🍃 **Infinitesimal:** Some tropical orchids have such minute (tiny) seeds that it would take 500 of them to equal the weight of a small flea. Being this small, they blow like dust through the air until landing on a moist surface where they can grow.

🍃 **Big flyer:** The seed of the Javan cucumber has wider wings than a monarch butterfly. With a wingspan of 5 inches (13 centimeters), it can glide in wide circles through the rain forest.

🍃 **Staying power:** A lotus seed found in a dry lake bed in China was discovered to be 1,300 years old. It actually sprouted when it was planted!

A Javan cucumber seed has paper thin wings.

Tapping the Earth

Most plants stay in one place for their entire life because they are rooted in the earth. As a seed sprouts and unfolds its cotyledon(s), the first root, known as a radicle, pushes down into the soil. By the time the first real leaves appear, the radicle has grown rootlets that are ready to tap the soil for water, oxygen, and nutrients.

Plants that will live just one season, such as tomato, watermelon, and pea plants, are called **annuals**. They stay alive for less than a year and depend on sprouting seeds for future generations. The roots of annuals are often shorter than roots of plants that live for two years (biennials) or longer (**perennials**). A common weedy annual called hedge parsley has shallow roots, which are small in comparison to the whole plant. Since it grows only during the wet season, its roots don't need to go very far to obtain water.

Most perennial plants have well-established roots to ensure a water supply during dry times and to store energy for new growth each year. In its first few months of growth, a manzanita shrub's roots may grow three or more feet long, while the stem above ground may be only a few inches tall. Many species of manzanita

The perennial marsh mallow plant has thick roots, which were used to make marshmallows before the recipe was modernized.

grow where there are dry seasons lasting up to half a year, and the long roots ensure that the plant will survive.

Mining the Soil

As a root grows hairs at its tip, it gets longer and pushes deeper into the soil. These hairs are about the same thickness of an average human hair and have a large surface area so they can easily absorb water. Roots produce and secrete, or give off, malic acid to help take in nutrients. Roots' hairs live only a few weeks. New ones are constantly

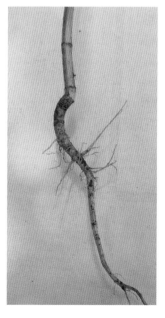

Like many annual plants, hedge parsley has short roots.

21

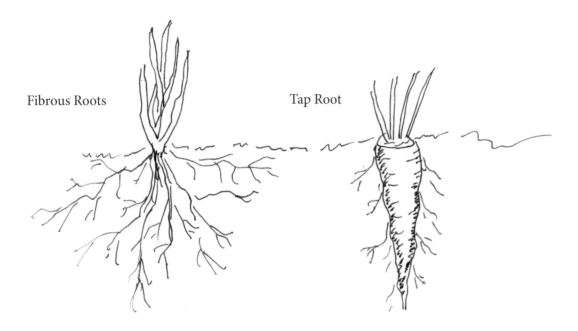

Fibrous Roots

Tap Root

- **Toy top:** Relatively flat and broad at both the top and middle and ending in a point, as in a turnip or sugar beet.
- **Spindle:** Tapered at the top and bottom and widest in the middle, as in a radish or beet.
- **Cone:** Widest at the top and gradually tapering toward the bottom, as in a carrot or parsnip.

Fibrous Roots

Grasses, tomatoes, and strawberries all have roots that divide into many fine branches beneath the surface.

growing near the root tip as the root gets longer. If these hairs are damaged, such as when transferring a seedling from a container to a garden bed, it will be more difficult for the plant to get water. So, it's best not to disturb the soil around a seedling.

The tip of each root has a cap that protects the growth cells and exudes a mucuslike substance to help the root slide through the soil. The cap, responding to gravity, guides the root downward past rocks and other obstructions in the soil.

Roots keep plants secured to the surface that they grow in. As roots weave their way into soil, they create a strong foundation that holds the aboveground plant parts in place.

Root Gallery: A Tour of Root Types

The two basic types of roots are taproots and fibrous roots. Within these two root types are special variations.

Taproots

Plants such as dandelions, carrots, and burdock have a single thick root, called a taproot, which grows deeply into the soil. Dandelion, carrot, and burdock roots store food for the plant and can also be eaten by people. Dandelion taproots grow up to four feet (1.2 meters) long. Taproots come in a variety of shapes:

Turnips roots are shaped like a toy top.

Custom Roots

- **Prop roots:** Tall corn plants can topple in wind or rain. For extra support, they can grow prop roots to hold them up with extra bracing. Mangroves growing along tidewater shorelines have prop roots called stilt roots. They keep the upper plant above the waterline.

- **Bacteria homes:** Specialized bacteria live in little globe-like lumps attached to some roots. They gather nitrogen gas from the air and transform it into ammonia, a nitrogen compound that plants use for growth. Most members of the pea family, which includes beans, clover, peanuts, and alfalfa, have root nodules containing nitrogen-fixing bacteria.

- **Anchors:** Many plants, especially garden vegetables and weeds, are annuals and live for only one season. Instead of the deep roots of perennials, they have short roots that both anchor the plant and provide water and nutrients.

Big sagebrush, the vegetation covering much of the vast and arid Great Basin of America's West, has both deep taproots, up to several meters long, and laterally

This maize has prop roots.

spreading roots along the surface. The roots of the two-foot-tall (0.6 meter) cholla, a type of cactus, can grow 30 feet (9 meters) deep, where the plant reaches water pockets far below the surface of the ground.

A towering saguaro cactus, which can grow seven stories tall, has shallow roots that spread out the same distance as the plant's height. These roots act as stabilizers during high winds. Shrubs growing in desert washes, where powerful flash floods can move boulders, are anchored by sturdy roots to hold them in place.

Rootless

When tiny pond creatures move near bladderwort, they might be sucked into a small

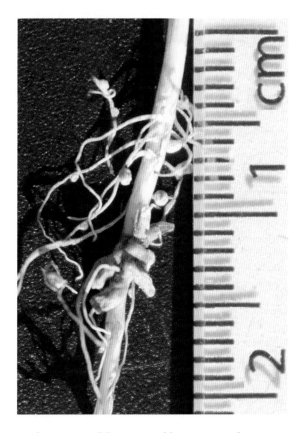

A clover root, like pea and bean roots, has nodules.

bladder where they are soon eaten. Clothed with feathery leaves, the bladderwort floats beneath the surface and, unlike most other vascular plants, lacks roots. Nutrients and water are absorbed through its finely lobed leaves.

Spanish moss, a relative of pineapples, grows on the surface of tree bark and rocks. Its hard wirelike "roots" act as grippers

ROOT DETECTIVE

Dig, shake, examine! Weeding can be a peaceful pastime, but it can be a chore when there are better things to do, like playing soccer or climbing a tree. Make weeding fun by becoming a root detective.

MATERIALS

- Spade or shovel
- White cardboard
- Magnifying glass
- Pen or pencil
- Plant journal

1. Dig up several different kinds of weeds by their roots and shake off the dirt.

2. Place the weeds on white cardboard and compare the root structures. Arrange the weeds with the same root structure side by side.

3. Use the magnifying glass to examine the roots for root hairs. If you find soil particles, critters, or fungus, jot down a few words to describe them in your plant journal. You also can write any questions that you have about the roots.

to hold tight to the surface, but they don't collect water or nutrients. The moss gathers these substances from the air, rain, and particles caught in the leaves.

Underground Pantry

Many biennial and perennial plants survive through a dormant season, when their aboveground parts lose leaves and sometimes appear dead. In very dry and cold regions, plants adapt to the harsh conditions by shutting down. Many of them store energy in roots underground and then use it for rapid regrowth the following season. These storage roots, called root **tubers**, are rich in starches. Both sweet potatoes and yams have tubers. Yam tubers can weigh more than 140 pounds (65 kilograms). Another plant with root tubers is the common four o'clock (*Mirabilis jalapa*), a vine that is planted in gardens and grows as a weed in Florida and Kenya. Manroot, a member of the squash family that grows in western North America, is named for its roots that can be the size of a small human or larger.

3

Plant Skeletons

When garden plants like tomatoes or beans die in autumn, all that remains are their skeletons. Unlike the skeletons of people and other vertebrate animals, which are made of bone, plant skeletons consist of the substances **lignin** and **cellulose**. Without skeletons, people would be as spineless as jellyfish. Plants without skeletons, like marine and freshwater algae, are limp and depend on water for support.

Stems and Branches

Land plants that depend on stems to provide their form and to help transport water and nutrients are called vascular land plants. *Vascular* means having veins, like

the veins we have in our bodies that carry blood.

Stems are the framework for a wide variety of forms, or postures. Just as some people stand erect while others stoop or slouch, plants also have many poses. Thyme sprawls like a green mat. Bedstraw clings. And sunflowers stand up like towers. Hedge parsley is spindly, while cabbages are squat. Ferns' fronds rise gracefully from underground stems called rhizomes. Strawberry plants lack stems but are connected to other strawberry plants by stringlike parts called **stolons**. Tomatoes have stems with numerous branches, while corn (maize) has a single unbranched stem. Spanish moss hangs like hair.

Pedal or Petiole

As you learn to ride a bicycle, you get to know the names of the specific parts, such as the frame, handlebars, chain, and pedals. Stem parts also have names:

- The main stem arises from the roots.

- Branches that come off this stem are called lateral stems, or petioles if they are thin stalks with a leaf attached at the end.

- A **node** is the point where the petiole or lateral stem is attached to the main stem.

- A stipule is a leaflike growth at the base of a stem.

(*above*) Cabbage leaves grow from a short stem.

(*left*) Sponge seaweed, like many other marine algae, lacks stems.

(*right*) Thistle skeletons are a common sight in autumn.

GO ON A PLANT FORM SCAVENGER HUNT

Tall, short, gangly, tubby! What plant forms adorn your neighborhood lawns and gardens?

MATERIALS

🕊 Plant journal
🕊 Pen or pencil
🕊 Camera (optional)

1. In your plant journal, write down the following plant forms: mat-like, squat, spindly, towerlike, rounded, tall and spreading, leaning, and climbing.

2. Now go on a scavenger hunt for each plant form. With a parent or guardian's permission, you can hunt in your neighborhood, local garden, or park. (If you can, arrange for a neighborhood or family gardener to join you.)

3. As you find each plant form, draw a picture of it in your journal or take a photo of it. Then jot down its location and name (if you know it) in your plant journal. You can later paste prints of photos in your journal.

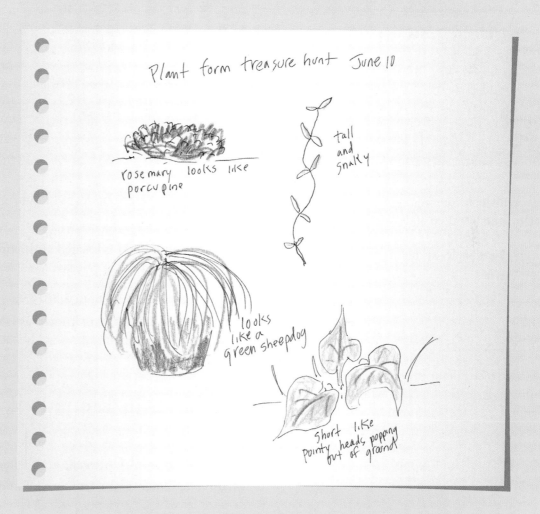

29

(*above*) People eat asparagus stems before the lateral and terminal buds open.

(*right*) New blades sprout from the tillers of barley grass.

- The zone between nodes is known as the internode.
- The terminal bud is located at the tip, or terminus, of the main stem.
- The buds along the stem, like those on an asparagus spear, are known as lateral buds.

Jack and the Beanstalk

A garden is an excellent place to observe how plants grow. A few weeks after a bean germinates, a new plant grows taller and taller as it climbs up a trellis or other support. The new leaves unfold at the uppermost tip. If you were watching a magic bean, like the one in the story "Jack and the Beanstalk," you would clearly see the plant growing from the top. Other plants, like tomatoes, sunflowers, and many other garden plants, also have a terminal bud, where new stem and leaf growth occur. If a caterpillar eats that bud, the lateral buds send out new growth. If a tomato plant is getting tall and spindly, gardeners will often pinch off the terminal buds to make the lateral buds grow. The result is a bushier plant.

Buds contain special cells that divide and produce new cells for the type of plant part required as the plant grows. Some of the cells in the terminal bud, also called the apical meristem, will develop new stem tissues while others will give birth to leaves.

Grasses are plants that evolved with grazing animals, such as bison or elk, continually munching them. Left ungrazed, grasses will develop stems that bear flowers. Grasses continually grow new leaves, called blades, from their bases. Unlike leaves on a tomato plant, these blades elongate from the bottom. Other blades grow rapidly from bundles of new leaves, folded inside a mature blade. Another source of new leaves is the crown, found at the base of a grass plant. From it sprout new stems, leaves, and special side stems called tillers, from which new blades emerge. When a lawn is mowed and a pasture grazed, the grass continues to grow. A row of beans that is mowed will stop growing. In cases of severe overgrazing, if the crown is eaten the grass doesn't grow back.

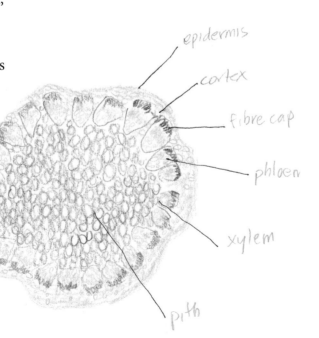

This cross section of a stem shows all its parts.

epidermis
cortex
fibre cap
phloem
xylem
pith

Green Plumbing– All About Stems

Whether short or tall, vertical or horizontal, all stems contain a system that delivers food, nutrients, and water throughout a plant.

Stems and Water

The water-carrying system known as the **xylem** is made up of dead cells that transport water flowing from the roots upward to all parts of the plant. Sugars, nutrients, and growth **hormones** move through a different plumbing system called the **phloem**.

MIND-BOGGLING BAMBOO

Bamboo is the largest plant in the grass family. Dragon bamboo can grow taller than a 10-story building. Giant bamboo, as its name implies, is the largest of over 1,000 species of bamboo. It can grow more than an inch an hour and up to three feet (1 meter) per day.

Bamboo is the fastest-growing plant in the world.

HOW DOES YOUR GARDEN GROW?

Plant, water, watch, and measure! This is a good outdoor activity for spring or summer. In winter, you can plant beans indoors in a ceramic or plastic pot filled with potting soil.

MATERIALS

- 2-foot-by-2-foot (0.6-meter-by-0.6-meter) plot in a garden, or a clay or plastic pot filled with potting soil
- Bean seeds
- Small watering can or large measuring cup
- Water
- Measuring tape
- Pen or pencil
- Plant journal

1. Make three holes in the soil with your index finger. The holes should be slightly deeper than the length of the beans.

2. Drop a bean into each hole and cover it with a few pinches of soil. Gently pat down the soil and sprinkle with enough water to make the top inch moist. For potted beans, also fill the plate underneath the pot with water.

3. Touch the soil daily. If it feels dry, sprinkle more water on it to keep the top inch of soil moist. The beans should sprout within a week.

4. Once they sprout, use the measuring tape to check their height every day and record it in your plant journal. For outside plants, jot down each day's weather conditions.

5. Keep measuring the sprouts for as many days as you want.

6. Review your notes. Which day had the greatest growth, and which had the least?

It is composed of living cells. In the xylem, water moves in only one direction, from the roots up. Fluids in the phloem move both from the roots upward and from the leaves downward.

Just like people, a stem is covered in skin called the epidermis. This skin may be hairy, waxy, thorny, rough, or smooth. Underneath the epidermis is the cortex, which both gives the stem strength and contains the xylem and phloem. The pith is in the center. Stems of perennial plants have bark on the outside and a woody cortex.

Water continually evaporates from the leaves of living plants in a process called **transpiration.** As water vapor exits the leaves, it is replaced by more water rising upward through the stems in a process called capillary action.

Sap-Tappers

Imagine poking a straw into a special plant and drinking a sweet meal rich in nutrients and sugars. Some insects have hollow beaks that can pierce a stem or leaf vein and then take in sap, like straws sucking up juice.

Think of a small hole in a garden hose. Can you picture a jetlike stream of water shooting out of the hole when the water is

 TRY THIS!

CELERY PIPES

Dip, wait, wonder! What happens when you place a celery stalk in water?

ADULT SUPERVISION REQUIRED

MATERIALS

- A short celery stem with leaves
- Knife
- Drinking glass
- Water
- Red or blue food coloring
- Magnifying glass
- Pen or pencil
- Plant journal

1. Ask an adult to help you cut off the bottom inch of the celery stem with a knife.

2. Fill the drinking glass halfway with water.

3. Place three drops of red or blue food coloring in the water.

4. Leave the stalk in the colored water for one day.

5. Use the magnifying glass to examine the bottom of the celery stem and the leaves for changes in color. What can you deduce about water transportation in plants from your examination? Record your observations in your plant journal.

6. Compare your celery stalk with the diagram of the celery stalk on this page.

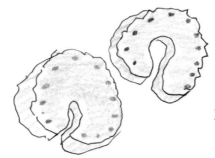

A cross section of a celery stem. Note the little dots along the edges; these are tubes for transporting water.

turned on? The same high-pressure release of liquid occurs when an insect makes a hole in the phloem of a plant. Without special adaptations, the insect would quickly fill up with sap until it burst.

Fortunately, this doesn't happen to animals that tap for sap. Aphids, common sap-feeding insects, have a specialized digestive system that partially digests the sap before releasing it through their anus (rear end). Drops of this excess sap, known as honeydew, coat leaves and the ground beneath the plant. Other insects, particularly ants, collect these honeydew drops as they ooze out from the rear of an aphid.

Called milking, this feeding habit provides an important food for ant colonies.

Scale insects, leafhoppers, and some species of caterpillars also produce honeydew. Leafhoppers, also known as sharpshooters, actually squirt honeydew. Hidden on stems under a mass of "spit" are spittlebugs, another sap-tapper that converts partially digested sap into frothy bubbles. Stinkbugs, harlequin bugs, and thorn bugs are other common insects that dine on sap.

In Asia and Mexico, lac scales, insects related to aphids, are raised on a variety of tree species. As the females pierce stems to feed on sap, they secrete a wax,

which conceals their bodies. For thousands of years people have harvested the wax-coated branches to extract the natural resin needed to make shellac, a substance used to protect the wood surfaces of musical instruments and furniture. As many as 20,000 tiny lac scales are needed to make enough waxy resin to produce a pound of shellac.

Some sap-tappers are feathered. A group of woodpeckers called sapsuckers pecks small holes in rows, known as wells, on trees and shrubs. They make the wells in both the xylem and the phloem of woody plants, and then they guard them from other sapsuckers. Hummingbirds and orioles feed from these wells.

Some sap-tappers actually eat toxic (poisonous) sap to protect themselves! The caterpillars of monarch butterflies feed on milkweed, which has sap that is toxic to most animals. The poisonous compound that is stored in their body tissue makes the caterpillars so distasteful that birds won't eat them. Another insect, the oleander aphid, is named for its ability to eat sap from the extremely poisonous oleander shrub. It can also feed on milkweeds. Like monarch butterflies, the oleander aphid has a bright color that alerts predators that it is inedible.

Ants collect drops of honeydew to bring back to their colony.

SAP-TAPPER DETECTIVE

Drip, squirt, spit, tap! Detecting sap-tappers requires a keen eye. Snoop about gardens and yards, paying special attention to stems and leaves. Aphids cling to the stems or leaf ribs. Be on the alert for gobs of spittle or bugs on stems.

MATERIALS

- Pen or pencil
- Plant journal
- Camera (optional)

1. Search for sap-tapping creatures on plant stems and the underside of leaves. Each time you locate a sap-tapper, sketch it in your plant journal or snap a photo of it. Later you can paste prints of your photos in your journal. Write down your observations as well; for example, "53 aphids on rose bush with lots of ants."

2. See how many different types of sap-tappers you can find in a half hour.

3. For the next week, keep an eye out for more sap-tappers. See if you can develop a special ability to find them.

4. Take a friend or family member to view your discoveries.

Elderberry shrubs lose leaves in winter.

Stem Life and Death

When annuals like tomato plants or corn die at the end of the season, a garden becomes a plant graveyard. The plants' stems may last until the following summer before they decay enough to become part of the soil.

Perennial plants such as blueberry or raspberry bushes develop woody stems that remain from year to year. In autumn they lose their leaves. Though they appear dead, in spring new growth will appear on these stems. When a perennial plant dies, its stems may take several years to decay.

All stems contain cellulose and lignin. Cellulose is the main component of the primary cell wall of green plants. Lignin makes cells more rigid and durable. It's most abundant in the bark and wood of perennial plants and helps move water through the xylem. Lignin, which decays more slowly than cellulose, is the last part of a woody stem or trunk to break down. The humus from rotted stems contains mostly lignin, which adds body to the soil and helps the soil absorb more water and oxygen.

Stems of plants like milkweed and flax have durable fibers that orioles and other birds gather for building their nests. The stems of plants like sunflowers have a soft center or pith. Some species of carpenter bees use pith to make the walls of nest cells in hollowed-out stems.

The Architecture of Stems

Forks, ladders, and arms: Stems branch in a variety of patterns. The side stems on mint and oregano plants are opposite from each other like the arms of an ape. Asparagus and nightshade branches arise from the main stem alternate from each other. Some side branches are close enough to be like a ladder. At the upper levels of a plant branches can divide into many parts, ending in a delicate forking of twigs. Most plants have an irregular, or asymmetric, pattern. This pattern may be the result of each plant's response to its unique location, like spiders that adapt their web structures to each site. How a plant branches is determined by its exposure to the sun and heat, the direction of strong winds, and its relation to neighboring plants that may block sunlight or limit growing space. It may be that no two plants, even of the same species, have identical branch patterns.

These Vietnamese women are harvesting sugarcane stalks to make cane sugar.

Stupendous Stems

Throughout the world people have discovered many uses for stems.

- **Sugar stem:** A grass called sugarcane, which grows in tropical regions such as the Caribbean Islands, has a thick stalk that is harvested to produce sugar. The stalks are milled to extract raw sugar, which is then made into white sugar.

- **Mud and wattle homes:** For thousands of years people have been building house walls from sticks woven together and plastered with mud. In tropical zones walls may simply be made from upright stems woven together with rope or vines.

- **Stick fences:** All over the world, people make fences for their livestock from sturdy sticks and vines. Some people also make fences from living plants. In parts of Mexico, people plant organ pipe cactus to create a wall that few animals or people want to squeeze through or climb over. Certain plants, such as species of shrub willow or acacia, are planted in tight rows to create a fence that not only keeps cows, goats, or other

LOOK FOR

FOLLOW THAT STEM

Which way do I go? Branches are highways for hunting insects like ladybugs. At each junction they take a turn right or left. In this activity your eyes will follow the highway system of a stem like a ladybug does.

MATERIALS

- Plant
- Pen or pencil
- Plant journal

1. Select a plant to observe. As your eyes travel up the plant's stem, take notice of each branch.

2. Carefully sketch the branches in your journal.

3. If the plant is small, such as a buttercup, sketch the entire plant in your journal. If it is a larger plant, such as a lilac bush, sketch one main stem up to its end branches.

The pads on your fingertips, palms, and undersides of your feet are covered with ridges. The pattern of these ridges is unique to each person. Prints made from people's finger pads, called fingerprints, are used for personal identification. Does each plant also have a unique branch pattern?

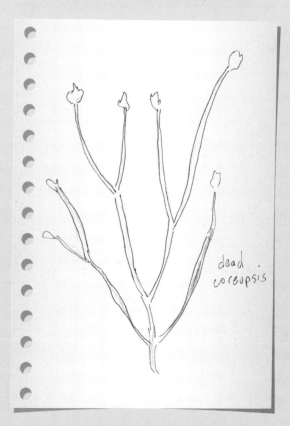

dead coreopsis

Sample drawing of a branch pattern.

livestock penned in, but also serves as a windbreak.

- **Box-branches:** A river begins with rivulets that join in streams and then merge into forks, which flow into the main stem of the river. In a plant, rootlets are connected to thicker roots that join a main root connected to the main stem of the plant. The main stem divides into side stems, which further split into twigs. A hydrangea leaf has a main vein that branches off in side veins, which then divide into smaller veins that reach the margin (edge) of the leaf. The branching of root stems and leaf veins helps liquids flow from a large area to a central point or from a central point to a large area. The veins in our bodies work the same way to move blood to our organs.

Hidden Pantry

Nibble, munch, crunch. Gophers and other subterranean (underground) creatures are constantly on the lookout for hidden plant pantries. Plants may store food for future growth in different types of storage stems.

- **Stem tubers:** Stem tubers are specialized stems used to store food for the next growing season. Potatoes, like other stem tubers, look like roots but have stem parts. When potatoes have been in the kitchen too long, they sprout white wiggly stems. The "eyes" of a potato are nodes, and each has a clearly visible leaf scar, and both are arranged in a spiral.

- **Bulbs:** Bulbs are another type of underground stem used to store food for future seasons. Tulips, onions, and garlic all have bulbs. The bulbs have a stem at the base, from which roots will grow down and leaves will grow upward in proper growing conditions.

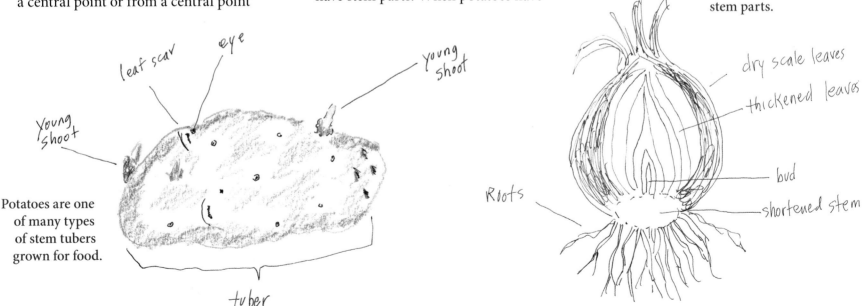

Potatoes are one of many types of stem tubers grown for food.

leaf scar   eye   young shoot

young shoot

tuber

Sliced onion with stem parts.

dry scale leaves

thickened leaves

bud

shortened stem

Roots

ROASTED ONIONS AND TATERS

Prep, bake, eat! Cook these edible underground plant stems and serve them to your family or friends. (Serves 4)

ADULT SUPERVISION REQUIRED

INGREDIENTS

- 3 medium potatoes
- ½ cup olive oil
- ½ teaspoon anise seeds
- ½ teaspoon dried rosemary or sage leaves
- ½ teaspoon salt
- ¼ teaspoon ground pepper
- Large red onion

MATERIALS

- Knife
- Cutting board
- Mixing bowl
- Spatula (heat-resistant)
- Large cookie sheet with rolled-up edges
- Oven mitts
- Serving platter
- Serving spoon

1. Preheat the oven to 400°F.

2. Wash and dry the potatoes.

3. Ask an adult to help you cut the potatoes into 1-inch (2.5 centimeter) cubes. Slide the cubes from the cutting board into a mixing bowl.

4. Add half (¼ cup) of the olive oil and all of the herbs, salt, and pepper. Stir the mixture with the spatula.

5. Use the spatula to scrape the potato mixture onto the cookie sheet.

6. Place the potatoes in the oven, stirring them with the spatula every 10 minutes. You'll bake them for a total of 30 minutes, but you'll prepare the onion while the potatoes are baking.

7. With an adult's help, cut the onion in half. Peel the skin off the onion halves.

8. Place the halves facedown on their flat sides and slice again lengthwise to make four equal chunks of onion.

9. Slice the quarter chunks crosswise into 1-inch-wide (2.5 centimeter) pieces.

10. Dump the onion pieces into the bowl you used for the potatoes.

11. Add the remaining ¼ cup of olive oil and mix.

12. The potatoes will be done when they are golden brown and easily pierced with a fork. Use oven mitts and ask an adult to help you remove the baking sheet from the oven and carefully transfer the hot potatoes to the bowl with the onions. Gently mix them together and then scrape the mixture back onto the cookie sheet. Bake for 10–20 more minutes until the onions are soft.

13. Place the roasted onions and potatoes on a platter with a spoon for serving.

14. Serve your creation to your guests.

Creeping rootstalks: Some plants, such as ginger, turmeric, and bamboo, have underground stems known as rhizomes. Like bulbs and stem tubers, rhizomes store starch, proteins, and nutrients the plant needs to send up new growth. The rhizome of a ginger plant has sections that can each grow a new plant.

Ginger rhizomes can be used fresh or in powdered form to flavor foods and beverages.

FRIED, MASHED, BOILED, OR BAKED

No matter how you prepare potatoes, they most certainly will fill your belly. Potatoes are an important source of calories for people throughout the world. An acre of potatoes yields more calories than an acre of corn (maize), wheat, or soybeans. First domesticated in the Andes Mountains of South America over 5,000 years ago, the potato became a staple food of the Inca and other ancient cultures. A grocery store would have to be massive to offer all of the world's 5,000 or more potato varieties. In India local varieties include *Phulwa* ("flowering in the plains") and *Gola* ("round potatoes"). The Andes has more than 3,000 varieties of potatoes, along with 200 wild species.

The first recipe for potato chips appeared in *The Cook's Oracle*, published in England in 1817. In it author William Kitchiner wrote, "Peel large potatoes, slice them about a quarter of an inch thick, or cut them in shavings round and round, as you would peel a lemon; dry them well in a clean cloth, and fry them in lard or dripping."

4

All About Leaves

The life of a leaf begins when a bud appears on the tip or nodes of a stem. Leaves will emerge when growing conditions such as day length, temperature, and moisture are just right. Within a few days they may reach their full size. These new leaves can live for months or even years.

(*left*) New leaves along the stem of a squash plant.

(*right*) Yucca leaves are stiff and sharp-tipped.

This pond lily leaf is round like a plate.

Green Wear

Clothed with leaves is a phrase to describe a plant in full leaf. If leaves are sort of like a plant's clothes, how would we describe the style of clothing? After all, leaves are as varied as human clothing. The foliage (covering of leaves) of a mullein is soft and fuzzy as velvet, while a thistle has a spiky punk-rocker outfit. Fern fronds are as lacy as a party dress. Yucca leaves are like a suit of armor. Just as there are hundreds of thousands of plants, there is an almost endless variety of leaves. Leaves can be smaller than a ladybug or as large as a beach umbrella.

Here are some other ways leaves vary:

🍃 **Texture:** Leaves can be as soft as silk, scratchy as sandpaper, slimy as a snail, or slippery as a slide. Some leaves sting. Others may cause a rash or poke skin.

🍃 **Shape:** If you asked someone to draw a picture of a leaf, would you expect it to be shaped like a heart, triangle, spear, needle, hand, eye, wheel, or fan? Would it have pointed or blunt tips? Be as thick as a thumb or as thin as a sheet of paper? In a garden you might spy Virginia creeper leaves with pointed tips or watermelon leaves with rounded lobes. Agave leaves are long and linear, while pond lily leaves are round.

- **Flavor: Warning—some leaves are poisonous and unsafe to eat.** A little bite of some leaves, such as those of poison hemlock, corn lily, and oleander, could be your last meal. Never eat a leaf before checking if it is edible. Of those leaves that *are* safe to munch, not all have the same flavor. Sorrel leaves are sour, and mustard leaves are spicy. Dandelion leaves are bitter, and spearmint leaves make a refreshing tangy tea.

- **Color:** Most leaves are green, but not all greens are the same—the dark green of holly, the pale green of a sweet potato leaf, and the bright green of parsley sprigs. Picture other shades of green you may have seen, ranging from the blue-green of broccoli to the gray-green of sage leaves and yellow-green of bamboo leaves. Coleus, a popular houseplant, is grown for its colorful red and green foliage. Spider plant, another common potted plant, has unique white-striped leaves. Many plants have leaves with a lighter shade of green on the underside. The upper side of a leaf has more chloroplasts, giving it a richer green appearance. In arid zones the underside of leaves may be coated with a dense mat of hairs to minimize water

WATCH WHAT YOU TASTE: COMMON POISONOUS LEAVES

Many leaves, such as lettuce, spinach, kale, and cabbage, appear on dinner tables throughout the world. You might not like the flavor of certain leafy vegetables, but at least they won't kill you. However, there are plenty of plants with deadly foliage that are best left alone.

- **Corn lily:** Though its large leaves look appealing to eat, don't be tempted. They can cause heart failure and eventually death.

- **Deadly nightshade:** Depending on the potency (power) of each plant, eating a single leaf can sicken or kill an adult. The roots are even more toxic.

- **Larkspur (delphinium):** The leaves of this pretty garden flower were once used to make poison arrows. After being struck by an arrow, the victim would experience nausea, then muscle twitching and paralysis before dying.

Its name alone indicates that deadly nightshade is lethal.

- **Oleander:** Every part of this common ornamental shrub is toxic. Eating any part could be fatal.

- **Poison hemlock:** Though it looks like a carrot plant, the red spots on the stem give it away as the carrot's infamous relative. Even a nibble can lead to a person's nervous system shutting down, which results in death.

Coleus leaves are very colorful.

Spinach has veins that branch like human veins.

loss. The hairs on horehound leaves give it a gray-green color. The underside of a bindweed leaf is brown, while that of chinquapin is yellow.

🌿 **Scent:** Plant scents evoke (bring up) different moods. The pleasant aroma of peppermint might conjure up memories of candy canes, while the savory scents of rosemary, thyme, and basil might help you recall a tasty meal. Lemon verbena is prized for its leaves that smell like lemon. Other plants, such as turpentine weed, have unpleasant-smelling foliage. The unmistakable aroma of onions and garlic comes from a potent sulfur compound in the leaves and other parts of the plant. **Volatile** oils—ones that easily turn to vapor—are the source of the scent of the desert-growing creosote bush, mints, and sage.

Leaf Anatomy

A dress shirt is composed of a set of parts that are sewn together, such as the collar, sleeves, cuffs, shoulder yoke, buttonholes, and buttons. A leaf is composed of parts as well. The main body of a

leaf is called the blade, which is equipped with veins. The veins may branch off from the midvein in dicotyledons, such as in spinach.

Monocotyledons like lilies, irises, and grass have parallel veins. The leaf edge, or margin, and the upper and lower surface have a layer of plant skin known as the epidermis. Most leaves, like those of geraniums and chickweed, are attached to the plant stem with a leaf stem called a petiole. A sessile leaf is one that lacks a petiole.

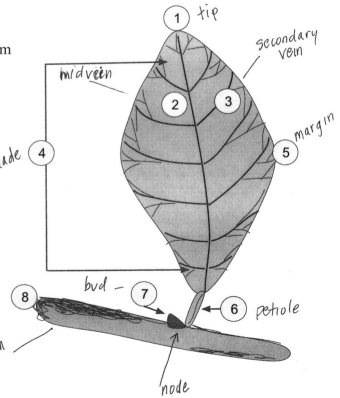

AROMARAMA

Sniff, inhale, take a whiff! Like a curious puppy, let your nose lead the way through a garden, meadow, or forest, in search of aromas.

MATERIALS

🌿 Pen or pencil

🌿 Plant journal

1. Select a leafy location rich in plants, such as a garden or natural landscape.

2. Sniff the air for any plant scents, and follow your nose to where they might be coming from.

3. Pick some leaves from the plants and gently bruise or tear each one before sniffing for a scent.

4. After you sample each leaf scent, jot down in your journal whether it has a noticeable smell. If it does, what does it smell like? For example, it might smell sweet, sour, or yucky. It might smell minty, spicy, or like licorice.

5. Collect some of the most aromatic leaves and bring them home to share with family or friends. Blindfolding them might help them smell the plants' scents better.

Dovecote geranium has undivided leaves that are fan-shaped with indented edges.

Leaf Styles

Leaves come in a wide variety of shapes. What can you find around your home?

🍃 Asters and spearmint have undivided, or entire, leaves. Violet leaves can be triangular.

🍃 Purple milkweed is one of many plants with heart-shaped leaves, while marsh marigold leaves are the shape of a kidney.

🍃 The margins are smooth on poison ivy, jagged on spearmint, and toothed on poison oak. Lobed leaves are blades with indented margins. The indentations can be shallow like those on the leaves of false dandelions or dovecote geranium, or almost reach the midvein in the case of California mustard. Leaves that look like hands, like those of thimbleberry, are called palmate.

🍃 Both strawberry and clover leaves have three leaflets. This kind of leaf made up of smaller leaflets is known as a compound leaf. A lupine leaf may have five to seven leaflets all attached to a central point, making it resemble a spider. The stem on a compound leaf, which bears each leaflet, is called a rachis. Like a simple leaf, it unfolds from a single leaf bud.

🍃 Compound leaves of a pea are referred to as pinnate due to their feather-like

LEAF PRINTS

Pick, tape, brush! When you use a leaf to make a print, each print will have a unique shape.

MATERIALS

- Leaves
- 1-inch-wide (2.5 centimeters) roll of masking tape
- Watercolor paper or card stock
- Broad-tip felt markers
- Watercolor or poster paints and paintbrush (optional)

1. Pick leaves from several different kinds of plants. Stiffer leaves are better because they won't rip easily.

2. Tear off small pieces of tape and make little rolls with the sticky side out.

3. Attach the tape rolls to one side of each leaf (longer leaves may need two or three rolls).

4. Place the leaf on the paper with the tape side down and gently press it to make it stick. Then add more leaves, leaving about 1 or 2 inches (2 to 5 centimeters) of space between.

5. Place your left forefinger (right if you are left-handed) in the center of one of the leaves to keep it in place.

6. With the broad side of the marker on the leaf, brush it from the middle toward the edge and repeat all the way around the margin of the leaf. It may work best to brush toward your body, so you'll have to rotate the paper to brush toward the opposite leaf edge.

7. For more delicate leaves from plants like dandelions or daisies, brush with watercolor or poster paint to avoid ripping them.

8. When you remove the leaves, you'll have a variety of colorful stenciled leaf shapes on the paper. Now that you know how to create leaf stencils, try decorating letters, cards, journals, or school folders with them!

Strawberry plants are easily recognized by their three leaflets with toothed margins. *Shutterstock*

appearance. Indigo leaves are called once pinnate because each leaflet is single. In plants such as parsley and cilantro, each leaflet is further divided into lobes. Pea leaves are attached alternate to each other on the rachis, while indigo leaves are opposite.

Well Clothed or Partly Naked

Plants may be "clothed" in leaves or almost bare. Leaves may grow only at the base of some plants, while other plants' leaves grow on the stems. Leaves of carrot, lettuce, or onion plants rise from ground level. Both dandelion and carrot leaves grow from a taproot, but dandelion leaves lie flat on the ground, while likely to suffer from dehydration or cold temperatures. Therefore, many plants in the far north, high mountains, and deserts grow low to the ground. If you have ever been outside when chilly winds are blowing, you might have rested like a log on the ground to avoid the cold. Certain alpine and desert plant species grow in dense cushions to minimize moisture loss and survive in low temperatures that slow photosynthesis. When these plants flower, the blossoms appear on a tall, flowering stem, like those on dandelions and carrots. Other plants growing in milder conditions, like common mallow or tomato plants, wear leaves up and down their stems.

Secret Solar Kitchens

Seaweed can photosynthesize in all its tissues, whereas land plants rely mostly on leaves for this process. Carbon dioxide, a gas, enters the leaves through microscopic mouthlike openings called stomata. Oxygen, also a gas, exits the leaves through these same pores.

A shrub called paloverde (Spanish for "green stick") has green trunks due to the presence of chlorophyll. Growing in deserts, where water is scarce, it sheds its small, feathery leaves during periods of drought. Even without the leaves it can photosynthesize using the chlorophyll in its trunks.

Through another process called respiration, plants use oxygen to oxidize, or break apart, sugar molecules. This releases the stored energy and forms carbon dioxide and water. During photosynthesis, plants produce and store energy in the form of sugar. Plants release this stored energy during respiration to grow and reproduce. Animals and other organisms, such as fungi, that can't produce their own food depend on plants for energy. This food energy is also released through respiration.

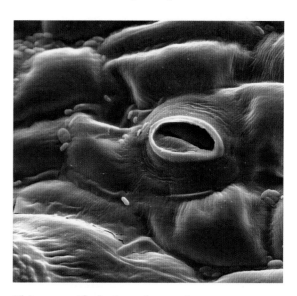

This magnified view shows the stomata on a tomato leaf.

FOG BREATH

Bag it and wait! On a cold morning you can see water vapor when you exhale outside. Living plants also expel water vapor—see for yourself!

MATERIALS

- 3 clear plastic bags (the kind used to bag fruits or vegetables)
- Bag ties
- Plant journal
- Pen or pencil

1. Choose a garden, vacant lot, or other site where your plants will not be disturbed.

2. Place a plastic bag over the tops of two different types of live plants and tie them tight around the stems.

3. Place a third plastic bag over the top of a dead plant or dead part of a plant and tie it tight around the stem.

4. In your journal jot down what you see through the bags. Record the time, date, and weather conditions.

5. Check the bags later in the day. Do you notice anything different?

6. Jot down what you see. The bags covering the living plants should be moist inside from water vapor produced during transpiration. The bag around the dead plant should be dry inside since a dead plant won't respire.

Seek the Light

Since green plants depend on sunlight to produce plant sugars, receiving the right amount sunlight is important. Phototropism is the action of a plant moving toward light. As the position of the sun changes during the day, plants such as cheeseweed and arroyo lupine turn their leaves to gain more sun exposure. At the top of a leaf stem, where it joins the blade, is a swelling called the pulvinus, which contains specialized plant cells. These cells enable a leaf to rotate to the best position. The individual leaflet of a lupine leaf is also able to fold and unfold during the day to regulate the amount of light striking its surface. It folds closed during intense light and heat to avoid water loss, and opens to maximize sun exposure early and late in the day.

Some leaves relax at bedtime. The leaves on some species of plants change position at the end of the day, such as those of false shamrock, also known as prayer plant. They droop at night and become upright in sunlight. As evening settles, the leaves of prayer plants rise.

The leaves of a mimosa, known as a sensitive plant, also close at night. But they also will fold up when touched, warmed, shaken, or even blown on. This action may help prevent its leaves from being eaten. Gnats or other small insects attracted to the sweet droplets on a sundew leaf are quickly trapped inside when the two halves of the leaf snap shut. After a few days, the plant digests these prey and absorbs their nutrients, and the leaf opens up again. The insects supply the plant with the nutrition it needs.

A Parade of Leaf Shapes

All leaves need to "breathe" in carbon dioxide, reduce water loss, and absorb the light energy needed for photosynthesis. Each species of plant is adapted to the environment where it lives. Many plants growing in the shaded, low-light understory of a forest have leaves with a large surface area to absorb sufficient sunlight. Those growing in direct sunlight receive enough sunlight, but the temperatures on the surface of their leaves can rise too high for maximum photosynthesis.

Just as fans provide relief to humans on hot days, breezes can lower leaf temperatures. Lobed leaves may cool faster than entire leaves because the distance from edge to edge is less. Lobes on leaves may also ensure better movement of water through veins to the leaf margins.

Leaves of plants in tropical rain forests are often wax coated, stiff, and slightly folded with a pointed tip. The waxy surface repels water, which is funneled off the leaf and flows off the tip to water the roots below.

Deer, mice, lizards, and rabbits can move from one place to another to avoid extreme heat or cold. A plant rooted in the ground can't crawl into a hole on a hot day or move to a sunny hilltop on a cold morning. Instead, a plant can alter the position of its leaves to face toward the sunlight or away from it. The leaves can fold or unfold along the midvein like some grass blades do when less water is available. By simply folding or curling, a leaf can lessen the amount of water it loses through its stomata.

Adaptable Leaves

Here are some other leaf influences and adaptations:

- **Size and number matters:** Domesticated cotton plants are the product of wild plants that were bred to produce

 TRY THIS!

SUN TRACKERS

Turn, sketch, wait, sketch again! Plants can't walk, run, or skip like kids. But can they move, slouch, or stand up straight?

MATERIALS

- Potted houseplant or potted seedlings
- Plant journal
- Pen or pencil

1. Place the plant next to a window for a full day. In your journal, sketch the posture of the plant. Is it standing up straight or leaning in one direction?

2. Check the plant in the afternoon of the next day. Look at your sketch to see if the posture is the same.

3. Sketch the plant once more and then turn the plant 180 degrees (halfway around).

4. Check the plant the afternoon of the following day. Compare its position with your last sketch. Has it moved? What direction is it facing?

larger amounts of cotton fiber. Wild plants have adapted to survive with less water and are more resistant to plant disease because they have a greater variety of leaf sizes and a smaller number of leaves per plant than farmed cotton has. When domesticated cotton plants interbreed with wild plants, the offspring have fewer leaves, and those leaves are both small and large. These changes increase the circulation of air through these plants, cooling the leaf surfaces. The tears along the edge of banana leaves serve a similar purpose in helping the plants survive through dry times.

- **The right amount:** Plants in dry locations have a variety of features that help them keep the small amount of water they do get. Plants in the deserts of Australia have stomata located in sunken pits on the leaf surface, where cool, damper air settles and reduces water loss. Many plants, such as sagebrush that grows in arid landscapes, have leaves coated with fine hairs to trap humid air. The smaller surface area of littler leaves found in plants such as thyme also helps to limit water loss. Plants can also suffer from too much water. One way plants can get rid of

A plant can release excess water from the edge of a leaf.

extra water is by guttation, the act of secreting droplets of sap from leaves.

- **Cold resistance:** Leaves can freeze if they are not equipped for cold weather. Thick leaves, like those of holly and yuccas, are resistant to frost. Low-growing plants like pachysandra and bearberry are short enough to be insulated from extreme cold by blankets of snow.

Cabbages, kale, and other mustard family plants contain chemical compounds that help them germinate during early spring and tolerate frost on their foliage. Leaves of rhododendrons curl downward to decrease the surface area exposed to cold temperatures, and the small surface area of needlelike rosemary leaves allows them to survive extreme heat and cold.

Leaf Eaters

If we had supersensitive hearing and stood in a field or garden, we would hear constant nibbling, munching, and crunching as thousands of plant-eating creatures nibbled, gobbled, and grazed on plants.

- **Munchers:** Gardeners are often upset when a gopher pulls a prized tomato or carrot plant into the ground. Rabbits are notorious for chomping lettuce and other vegetables. Huge tomato hornworms devour stems, fruits, and leaves, leaving behind only their droppings as a clue of their presence.

Leaf chafers, earwigs, grasshoppers, katydids, and crickets also dine on leaves for breakfast, lunch, and dinner. Horses, sheep, cattle, and other grazers mow pasture plants as they chomp and chew grasses and forbs.

- **Special diets:** Many species in the leaf beetle family are named for the plants they consume. Among them are asparagus, potato, cucumber, and bean leaf beetles. A large group of butterfly-like insects called skippers feed primarily on grass. Caterpillars in particular are known for feeding primarily on plants in a single plant family. Caterpillars of cabbage butterflies eat leaves of cabbage family plants such as broccoli, mustard, and radishes, while caterpillars of checkerspot butterflies prefer greens from snapdragon family plants. Sod webworms are moth caterpillars that feed on turf.

- **Picky eaters:** Caterpillars, like that of the grape leaf skeletonizer, are named for their habit of eating all of a leaf except for the skeleton-like veins. The leaves of raspberry plants are also eaten in this way by a beetle grub called the raspberry fruitworm. Skeletonized leaves look like lace.

- **Miners:** Some fly, wasp, and moth larvae eat inside leaves, between the upper and lower epidermis where they are protected from predators. The meandering lines left by these miners look like scribbles or white blotches.

- **Rollers and folders:** Bean leaf and redbud leaf rollers make a safe haven from predators by rolling leaves and using silk to make tubes. Similarly, a grape leaf folder ties a folded leaf with silk.

- **Gall makers:** Female sawflies (a type of wasp), gall wasps, mites, aphids, and small flies called midges are among the 1,500 species of invertebrates that create growths on leaves called galls. Soon after a female gall wasp inserts eggs into a leaf, a tumorlike growth, called a gall, develops. Inside these galls, larvae benefit from the safe shelter packed with nutritious food. Scientists think that chemicals, viruses, or a physical change in plant cells may trigger the growth of galls.

- **Leaf cutters:** Animals depend on leaves for more than food. Leaf-cutter bees use their jaws to slice round pieces of leaf, which they use to build partitions on their ground nests. A long line of

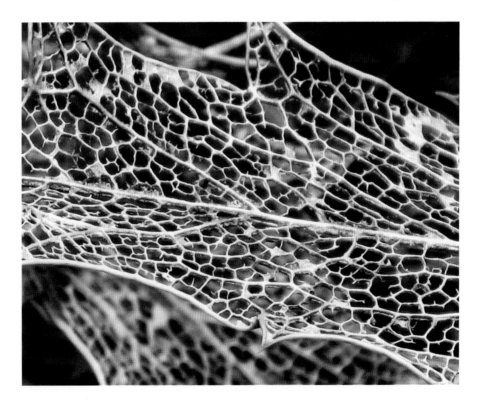

The caterpillar that dined on this thistle leaf ate everything but the veins.

ants carrying pieces of leaves is a common sight in tropical regions. The ants haul the specially cut leaf fragments to their colony to provide nutrients for the fungus gardens that they depend on for food.

Leaf Me Alone: Plant Defenses

Plants may seem like sitting ducks, just waiting helplessly for plant-eating animals to nibble their leaves. Plants can't run and hide, but they can defend themselves.

- **Spines, prickles, hairs, and thorns:** Have you ever been snagged by a sharp thorn while picking blackberries, or been poked by a spiny thistle? The spines on a thistle, prickles on a raspberry stem, and thorns on a rose stem discourage most livestock and other mammal herbivores (plant eaters) from eating the plants.

  If you look at a bush bean leaf with a magnifying glass, you'll see small hairs that look harmless. But like spikes once used to defend castles, these hairs defend the bean leaves against invaders. The leaves' hooked hairs are sharp enough to impale small caterpillars.

Soybean leaves have a dense coating of hairs that acts like a wall to prevent hatching insects from reaching the fleshy part of the leaf.

- **Yuck, gag, pucker!** Many plants deter herbivores by simply tasting terrible. Caffeine, found in coffee and tea plants, is not only bitter but also can block reproduction in insects as well as be toxic to fungi. The high level of caffeine in coffee seedlings can prevent the germination of seeds of other plants, ensuring that they have less competition from other plants.

  Certain plants produce large amounts of compounds called tannins that not only make the leaves bitter but also prevent insects that eat a lot of tannins from gaining weight. As a result, the insects eventually die. In other plants, alkaloids serve the same purpose. Only a few caterpillar species, such as the tomato hornworm, are able to ingest the alkaloids and other chemicals in tomato and potato leaves.

  Lupines, a common plant in the pea family, contain lupin, a bitter-tasting and mildly toxic alkaloid substance. Livestock avoid eating lupines. Unfortunately, when their pastures are overgrazed and lupine is the only available food source, livestock may get sick or die from eating large amounts of lupine. The same is true for iris, larkspur, and other poisonous plants. If consumed in large quantities by hungry cattle or sheep, they may cause death.

- **Cry and scram:** Slicing an onion releases a sulfur gas that makes cooks cry. This gas also repels any creature that bites into onion, garlic, or leek plants. When onions are cooked, their sulfur defenses are deactivated.

- **Grow up, shed, grow another head!** Spinach leaves lack a chemical compound that grasshoppers need to develop into adults. After their first meal of spinach, somehow they know to avoid it.

  Mexican paintbrush contains one chemical that triggers immature insects to shed their skins prematurely, which often kills them. It has another substance that prevents insect eggs from hatching.

  In the leaves of bugleweed is a compound that mimics a caterpillar hormone. After munching the leaves, caterpillars develop into pupa with multiple heads.

Choose your poison: Poison is the defense of choice for many plants. Birdsfoot trefoil and Johnsongrass use toxic cyanide compounds to deter leaf-eating insects. A dose of hydrogen cyanide is so deadly it can kill a human in less than a minute.

Many members of the cabbage family release a poison "mustard" gas to fend off grazers. Toxins in foxglove can cause heart attacks in rabbits, chickens, and other vertebrates. Milkweed also contains compounds that can interfere with heart functions. Milkweed bugs and the caterpillars of the monarch butterfly are immune to the toxins in milkweed. They store the poison in their bodies, which makes them distasteful to birds.

The castor bean plant contains a powerful poison called ricin. A tiny amount can kill a large animal. Aphids perish within a day after sipping the sap of this plant. Like the monarch caterpillar, the caterpillar of the croton moth is resistant to the toxin and in turn becomes toxic.

Invisible commands: Imagine having a weapon that could make your attackers follow your command! Lima bean and cotton give off a substance that signals parasitic wasps to attack the insects eating their leaves. Leaves of lima bean plants that are being eaten by spider mites release a chemical that attracts predatory mites. Specialized hairs on tomato and potato plants ooze oils that make aphids go away.

Attack of the cells: Crazy cells (known as idioblasts) hide amid normal cells, waiting, like superheroes, to leap into action when an unsuspecting creature takes a bite. Filled with tannins, the cells rapidly ruin the taste of the meal.

Do not be dumb—do *not* taste dumb cane!

Stone cells can wear down an insect's jaws. One tropical plant called dumb cane (dumb as in "unable to speak"), which is often grown as a houseplant, earned its name from the presence of crystal cells packed with sharp calcium oxalate crystals. To an insect, taking a bite of the plant is like chewing broken glass. When people or pets chew leaves of dumb cane, they may experience a burning sensation in their mouth and throat, followed by inflammation, choking, and difficulty speaking.

- **Lying in wait:** Chemicals in plants also defend against bacterial and fungal diseases. In some plant species, defensive chemicals are present at all times, while in others their production is triggered by the saliva of munching insects.

Ouch, Itch, Burn

Don't learn the hard way! Keep your distance from these unpleasant plants.

- **Don't meddle with nettles:** An encounter with a nettle plant can test your mettle, or strength. Covering its leaves and stems are thousands of hollow hairs with cells that act like hypodermic needles. When bare skin touches these hairs, they inject toxins that feel like a bee or wasp sting. And the pain gets worse before it fades away. Prostaglandin, a hormone that stimulates pain receptors in the skin, intensifies the sense of pain.

- **Poison oak is no joke:** Coating poison oak leaves and stems and ivy leaves is an oil called urushiol. The danger of brushing bare skin or clothes against it is not evident until a few hours—or even a whole day—later, when a rash appears on the skin. The rash can be mildly irritating or erupt into a mass of oozing, extremely itchy sores that may take more than a week to disappear. People vary in their sensitivity to urushiol. The oil is particularly potent in smoke from burning leaves or stems and can cause internal rashes that can be quite serious. Squirrels, wood rats, sapsuckers, robins, and other birds eat poison oak berries with no ill effects.

- **Giant hogweed:** Don't be a sap and let your bare skin come in contact with sap from this plant. Sunlight makes this sap toxic to skin, causing it to become red and itchy. Within two days the "burn" may blister and leave long-lasting scars. Even a small amount of sap coming in contact with eyes can lead to temporary or permanent blindness. Native to the Caucasus Mountains, giant hogweed has spread into many parts of northern Europe, Canada, and the northeastern and northwestern United States. Fortunately, it is easy to recognize. As its name implies, this plant is big, growing more than seven feet (2 meters) tall.

- **Tread lightly:** Walk carefully in pine and oak forests of the southeastern United States, where the plant called tread lightly grows naturally within the boundaries of nine states. Growing on the forest floor, it is easy to miss unless you touch it. It has several different names, including tread lightly, spurge nettle, and finger rot. Each name warns that it is a plant to avoid. Touching its stinging hairs with bare skin results in pain, swelling, and red pimples on the upper body parts that can last for several days. Eating it causes immediate vomiting and unconsciousness. Many of its relatives in the spurge or Euphorbia family have toxic sap that can cause painful inflammation.

Plants with toxic substances have been used for centuries in both ancient

Chinese and Indian medicine. Pharmaceutical researchers are investigating them to treat ailments ranging from precancerous skin conditions to diabetes.

Unleaved

Not all plants have leaves. Broomrape doesn't need leaves because it is a parasite that takes food from the roots of other plants. Snow plant also lacks leaves. It obtains food from soil fungi.

Big Banana Leaves

Most people think bananas grow on trees, but the banana plant is actually a very large herb. Unlike a tree, the main stem is not woody and not even a real stem. The banana plant is a pseudostem (*pseudo* means "false"). It is made up of tightly packed leaf sheaths, which are the widened lower part of the leaf stem. Large leaves unfurl from each of these stems. Over time the leaves die, but the underground stem, known as a corm, can live for decades, sending up shoot after shoot. Banana plants are the largest herbs. They grow up to 40 feet (12 meters) tall and have the biggest leaves of any herb.

5

Flowers and Petals, Birds and Bees

With their bright colors, fantastic shapes, and lovely fragrances, it's no wonder that flowers grab our attention and imagination. Known by fanciful names, such as buttercup and snapdragon, flowers grace gardens, planter boxes, and fields. Though the variety of shapes, sizes, and colors is mind-boggling, flowers are more than pretty ornaments. They are essential to the future of every plant.

Flower Anatomy

PETAL

stigma

STAMEN { stamen
filament

style

PISTIL

ovary

sepal

STEM

Like bright neon signs, petals catch our sight. Other flower parts are less noticeable. Underneath the showy petals is a green leaflike part called a **sepal**, which is often triangular in shape. In the very center of a flower are the **pistils**, the female part of a flower, which shelter eggs in the **ovary** at their base. Circling the pistils are the **stamens**, the male part of a flower, which bear pollen. Each of these parts plays a role in reproduction because flowers continue the existence of every species of flowering plant.

The number of petals on a flower can vary. They can be large or small, wide or narrow. The special characteristics of a flower's petals are important in identifying different species. For example, western buttercups have five petals, while California buttercups have many more. A mariposa lily has three petals, but an evening primrose has four. A cucumber flower also has five petals.

A Rainbow of Petals

Pink, red, magenta, baby blue, sky blue, royal blue, purple, violet, and mauve. White, creamy yellow, sun yellow, golden,

Count the petals to find out which one is a western buttercup and which one is a California buttercup.

PETAL NUMBERS

Three, four, five, many more! Conduct a census of petals.

MATERIALS

- Magnifying glass
- Colored pencils
- Plant journal

1. Visit a garden, vacant lot, field, or forest where there are a variety of flowers.

2. Count the number of petals on as many different kinds of flowers as you can find. Use a magnifying glass to examine small flowers. Make a simple sketch of each flower in your plant journal.

3. Is there a petal number that seems to be the most common?

4. As you survey the flowers, notice the petals. Petals have many different shapes. You might see teardrops, hearts, paddles, and triangles! What shapes can you discover?

Crown of thorns is unusual because it has only two petals per flower.

With their cardinal red color, cardinal flowers are easily spotted on the forest floor.

orange, burnt orange, and reddish-brown. The colors of petals pop out like bright billboards among the rich greens of leaves and stems. Flowers such as baby blue eyes, red maids, cardinal flowers, goldenrod, and cream cups are named for their colors.

CONFUSING CULTIVARS

Over centuries, many wild plants have been specially bred to produce larger or more flavorful seeds or fruits, or bigger and showier flowers. Most garden roses are **cultivars**, which means they are carefully bred to look a certain way. For example, garden roses have many more petals per flower than wild woodland roses have. Cultivars are also bred in colors not seen in their wild ancestors.

Wild roses have five petals, whereas a rose cultivar like this one is bred to have many. *Shutterstock*

PETAL COLORS

Blue or purple, red or pink, orange or yellow, white or lavender: colors abound in flowerbeds and gardens. Which petal colors can you find in your neighborhood?

MATERIALS

- Paint sample cards (available at paint or hardware stores)
- Magnifying glass
- Pencil
- Plant journal

1. Visit a garden, vacant lot, field, or forest where there are a variety of flowers.

2. Try to match the colors of petals on as many different kinds of flowers as you can with the colors on the paint sample cards. Use a magnifying glass to examine tiny flowers. Do some petals have more than one color? How many have different shades of one color? Does a certain color seem to be the most common?

3. Sketch one of the flowers in your plant journal and jot down the name of the color or colors from the cards that most closely match the petals. Repeat with more flowers.

How Pollination Works

A close look into a flower reveals a set of strange-looking structures. In the very center you'll find torpedo-shaped female parts called pistils. At the tip is the stigma, attached at the top of a column called the style, which rests on the pedestal-like ovary. Protected within the ovary are **ovules**, or eggs. Standing in a ring around the center are pillow-like packages on stilts, called stamens. When stamens are mature, the pillows, called anthers, open to reveal pollen grains. Pistils and stamens are the reproductive organs of the plant part, known as the flower.

Flowers with colorful petals act like advertisements for many different pollinators, including birds, bees, beetles, butterflies, bats, moths, flies, and wasps that help transfer pollen from one flower to another. To humans, flowers are symbols of purity, beauty, and love. To pollinators, they are restaurants.

Flowers that rely on wind to carry pollen lack petals. Instead, they have dangling stamens that release pollen with the help of a breeze and feathery pistils ready to catch wind-borne pollen.

Pollen

A pollen grain is like a small space capsule with two passengers inside. These pollen-nauts are male sex cells, called gametes. They have the important mission of fertilizing an egg of the same species of plant. The capsule is specially designed to carry out this task. Its tough outside layer serves as a shield that protects the gametes riding inside from the harsh conditions outside, such as dry air and intense solar radiation. The surface of the pollen grains of animal-pollinated flowers are covered in devices, hooks, depressions, or cavities to ensure the grain adheres to the body of the pollinator, helping the mission. On the other hand, pollen grains that depend on wind for transport are dish or parachute shaped,

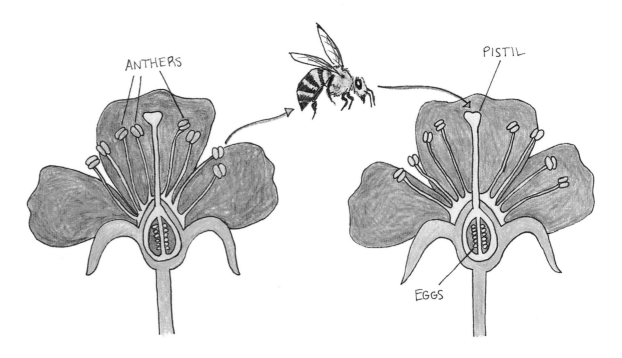

allowing them to be carried like small kites by soft breezes or strong gusts.

Mission Accomplished

When a pollen grain, whether carried by wind or a pollinator, ends up on the stigma of a ripe pistil, an amazing event occurs. One of the cells in the pollen grain uses food from the stigma to grow into a tube. This tube is sometimes thousands of times bigger than the size of the grain. The tube threads its way like a worm down through the style and into the ovary. Once in the ovary its tip enters a single egg, called an

The pollen grains are visible on the ripe anthers of this tulip.

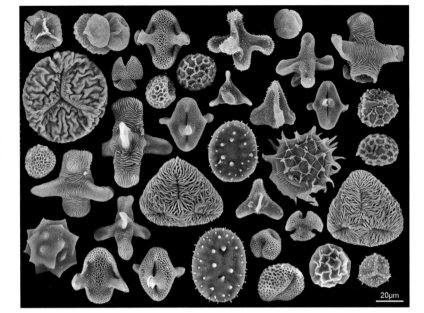

These fantastic shapes and surfaces of pollen grains are visible only through a powerful microscope.

20µm

ovule. Meanwhile, the other cell inside the pollen grain splits into two sperm cells and both descend through the tube to the egg. One sperm fertilizes the egg to form an embryo. The other becomes the endosperm, a food source for the developing embryo and future sprout.

Flower Design

At first glimpse all flowers look similar, but on closer inspection you can see some major differences.

- **Male, female, or both?** A buttercup and strawberry flower have both male and female parts. In each of these flowers the pistils are in the center, surrounded by many stamens. A cucumber plant, however, has some flowers that are female, containing only pistils, and others that are male, containing only stamens. Botanists call flowers that have both stamens and pistils *perfect* and ones with just male or female flowers *imperfect*. Some plants, such as nettles, pussy-toes, or meadow rue, are strictly male or female. One plant has flowers with only pistils, and another has flowers with only stamens. A species with male and female plants is called

TOUGH COATS

The outer jacket of pollen is extremely resistant to decay, enabling pollen grains to stay undamaged for centuries. Each species of flowering plant pollen has unique characteristics that help experts identify pollen grains. Pollen grains washed into a lake or other body of water may be buried in the sediments on the bottom. When scientists take samples from ancient sediments or glacial ice, they can identify the pollen and get clues about what plants grew at the time when the sediments were deposited or the ice formed. Since each plant requires a special set of climatic conditions, such as warm temperatures and lots of moisture, to grow, the type of plants identified by the pollen reveals the climate that existed at a particular time. This helps scientists understand how climate has changed.

dioecious (*di-* means "two" and *oecious* means "home" in Greek).

- **Separate or joined?** A flower can have separate petals like those of a poppy or ones that are fused together like a potato flower. The petals may be fused to form a tube as in morning glory flowers.

- **Same or different?** Each petal of a single mustard, potato, or poppy flower is the same shape and size, while the petals of violet, snapdragon, or honeysuckle flowers vary in shape and size. In both violets and snapdragons, the longer lower petal serves as a landing platform for visiting pollinators.

A Pollination Story

Picture a buttercup blossom growing in a lawn under the shade of a leafy tree. In its center are developing pistils, not yet ready to receive pollen. Surrounding the pistils are ripened stamens bearing anthers bursting with pollen. A small bee lands, laps up nectar, and flies off with pollen stuck to its body. It lands next on a buttercup growing in the bright sunshine. This buttercup started blooming many days earlier and its pollen is gone, but the stigmas are enlarged and ready to accept pollen. A pollen grain delivered by the bee rubs off onto one of the stigmas and soon fertilizes an egg below, inside the ovary. The developing seed will have **genes** from both the sun-loving and shade-loving flower.

In every garden, meadow, forest, and field this story takes place over and over again. The pollinator, whether it is a bee, butterfly, or beetle, visits flowers seeking food and in exchange transfers genes ensuring that future plant populations

(*left*) The five petals of a potato flower are fused together.

(*right*) The upper and lower petals of a violet are slightly different in size and shape.

FLOWER SHAPES

Is it a pinwheel, a trumpet, a mouth, a cross, or a star? Examine and sketch the shapes of various flowers.

MATERIALS
- 🐦 Colored pencils or markers
- 🐦 Plant journal

1. Visit a garden, a landscaped area around a school or building, a field of flowers, or a forest where there are a variety of flowers.

2. As you look at each flower, think of what its shape looks like. Many of the common names of flowers refer to a flower's shape. For example, monkeyflower looks like the face of a monkey, woodland star is star shaped, bleeding hearts look like a heart that has burst, and sunflowers look like a kid's drawing of the sun.

3. Sketch each flower in your plant journal and give it a name based on its shape.

will have the rich array of characteristics preparing them for changes in their environment. The world is constantly changing. Climates change from hot to cold and wet to dry. Changes in soils, plant-eating insects, and diseases determine which plants will be most likely to survive and pass on their unique characteristics.

A Gallery of Pollinators

Insect-pollinated flowers are generally every color except bright red. Most insects view the world differently than we do.

Instead of seeing colors in visible light (the light that people and other vertebrate animals can see), they view colors in the ultraviolet light range. In this range of light, red is not visible. Insects can see purple-red or brownish-red, but not pure red. Red flowers are usually pollinated by hummingbirds or sunbirds. Here is a gallery of insect pollinators.

- 🍃 **Beetles:** Among the million-plus species of beetles, many are important pollinators. The flowers of cow parsnip and Queen Anne's lace are filled with tiny soft-winged flower beetles eating nectar and pollen. The colorful mariposa lily blooms just in time to be pollinated by long-horned beetles, who spend most of their life as grubs in dead trees before emerging as adults. Checkered beetles visit flowers to eat small pollinators and also help pollinate the flower. The tumbling flower beetle is another common pollinator known for its ability to turn while it jumps and escapes from predators.

- 🍃 **Flies:** The annoying housefly that buzzes around inside homes is just one of more than 160,000 species of flies.

Many species of flies are important pollinators. Some, like bee flies and hoverflies, also known as flowerflies, are often confused with bees. Hoverflies have a striped pattern like a bee, and bee flies are fuzzy like bumblebees, but both can hover while feeding on flowers, something bees can't do. Flowerflies are second only to bees in pollinating the flowers of crops. Some of the metallic blue or green small-headed flies have long tongues that can reach to the bottom of inch-deep flower tubes to lap up nectar. Male mosquitoes, members of the fly family, pollinate orchids. Half of the fly families include species that pollinate flowers. Sometimes blossoms, like those of wild carrot or parsnip, are filled with march flies and gnats. Fruit flies that eat decaying fruit are attracted to flowers that smell rotten, and flies that lay eggs in decaying matter are attracted to other flowers that have a rotten odor.

Butterflies and moths: When a caterpillar transforms from a creature with leaf-munching jaws into a butterfly or moth, it must have flowers to sip from with its nicely coiled straw-like mouth.

Bee flies can be distinguished from bees by their long tongues and hovering flight.

LOOK FOR

PETAL PATTERNS

Plant petals vary not only in color and shape, but also in their patterns, such as rings, spots, lines, and other markings. Some of these patterns help in the plant's reproduction. For example, forget-me-nots have a color pattern similar to the bull's-eye on a target. This pattern indicates the center of the flower, where the pollinator should insert its tongue. Violets have guidelines on the lower petals that lead right to the throat of the flower, where the nectar is found. Foxglove has spots that serve the same function.

MATERIALS

🖋 Colored pencils or markers
🖋 Plant journal

1. Visit a garden, a landscaped area around a school or building, a field of flowers, or a forest where there are a variety of flowers.

2. Examine any patterns you notice on the flower petals.

3. Draw some of the patterns you find. Do you ever see these patterns elsewhere in nature? In art? On fabrics or textiles? Record your thoughts in your plant journal.

Upon landing on a flower, a moth or butterfly straightens its tongue and inserts it in a flower. Picture a large yellow swallowtail butterfly or a tiny fairy moth coiling and uncoiling its tongue, also called a proboscis, thousands of times a day as it feeds on hundreds of flowers. Moths generally prefer white, pale yellow, or blue flowers. Butterflies feed on white, yellow, blue, and purple flowers.

Some moths, such as the sphinx moth, specialize in pollinating tubular flowers while hovering and inserting their proboscis.

Busy bees: When most people picture a bee, they see a honeybee or bumblebee, but those are just two of the many kinds of bees. Among the more than 20,000 species of bees are the tiny miner bee (*Perdita minima*), which is not much larger than a sesame seed, and the largest, the mason bee, which is as big as a peach pit. Most bee species are solitary, unlike honeybees and bumblebees, which live in hives. Female solitary bees collect pollen and deposit balls of pollen in a burrow, which they seal off after laying their eggs.

Bee time: Bumblebees are one of the most important pollinators in the cool regions of the world. Their ability to raise their body temperature allows them to fly during cold weather. Flowers dependent on bumblebees produce more nectar on cold days to provide

(*above*) Checkerspot butterfly.

(*left*) Sweat bees are named for their habit of sopping salt from sweaty skin.

(*right*) Bees visit flowers with a wide range of colors, including pink, blue, purple, yellow, orange, and white.

them with the extra energy needed to fly in such conditions. Bumblebees and honeybees can tell time. Because many species of flowers rely on bumblebees, each of these flower species can produce nectar at a certain time to ensure the bumblebees' exclusive services during that period.

Bee flowers may be tubular like mint, tiny like thyme, large like sunflowers, or open like strawberry blossoms.

Flower Friends with Skeletons

Bats, birds, and even a lizard also pollinate flowers!

- **Bats:** The giant saguaro and organ pipe cactus, as well as many species of agave, depend on lesser long-nosed and Mexican long-nosed bats for pollination. These two species live in southern Arizona and New Mexico and Central America. Flying through the desert night, they visit large white night-blooming flowers. Throughout the world, mostly in the tropics of the Americas, Africa, and Asia, bats are responsible for pollinating over 500 species of plants, most of which are white and have a musky odor.

PEA FLOWERS

Lupines and many other pea family flowers have a specialized flower that is only pollinated by bees. These flowers have a large upper petal, called the banner, that serves as a billboard signaling the bee to visit. Below it are two sail-like petals that act as landing pads.

Small bees, such as sweat bees, visit small flower lupines, while medium-sized leaf-cutter bees visit medium-sized lupine flowers, and bumblebees visit the largest. When the correct size bee rests on a lupine flower, its weight forces the sail petals downward, causing the bee to touch the folded petal hidden underneath.

From the folded petal of fresh flowers at the top of the stem, the stamens pop out and powder the bee with ripe pollen. From the folded petal of older flowers toward the bottom of the stem, the pistil pops out and picks up pollen from another lupine the bee has visited. As the flowers age, the spot on the banner changes color, usually becoming purple. This tells the bees that there is more nectar in them. Thus bees start at the bottom of the flower stalk and make their way upward.

As the bee lands on the lower petals of a pea flower, the pistil is sprung upward into contact with its body.

- **Birds and blossoms:** Hummingbirds and sunbirds are two groups that specialize in feeding from flowers. Sunbirds live in Africa, Asia, Australia, the Middle East, and Egypt, while hummingbirds live only in the Americas. Both groups are the exclusive pollinators of flowers such as red columbine, bright red paintbrushes, fuchsias, and other tubular red flowers. Bird-pollinated flowers have concentrated nectar that supplies the birds with enough energy to fly from blossom to blossom.

- **Gecko:** In tropical zones there are few flowers that depend on the gecko, a smooth-skinned climbing lizard, for pollination.

Tiny Pollinators

Adult butterflies, bee flies, and bees depend on flowers for food, but they rely on other foods as larvae. Other smaller nectar eaters, such as parasitic wasps, also count on flowers for survival. In its larval stage the wasp lives inside the body of a caterpillar, beetle grub, aphid, or fly maggot. It eats the insides of the host while keeping it alive until the larvae is ready to turn into a pupa. By the time it makes a cocoon, the host is a dead shell. When the winged adult wasp emerges, it feeds on nectar and seeks a mate. Then the mated females deposit eggs in a suitable host.

Many species of these parasitic wasps only lay eggs in a single species of host. For example, one wasp species lays eggs only in tomato hornworms while another species lays its eggs in cabbage white butterfly caterpillars. These wasps are known as parasitoids, because unlike bedbugs or ticks, they eventually kill their host. Even smaller parasitic wasps, some the size of the period at the end of this sentence, parasitize the eggs or larvae of larger parasitic wasps. Many pollinate tiny flowers in the carrot family, and some have been found on orchids. Those that kill caterpillars or other insects that eat plants are important in controlling insects that farmers consider to be pests.

Perfect Partners

In North America an amazing relationship exists between yucca plants and the tiny yucca moth. After mating with a male moth, the female yucca moth flies to a yucca flower and scrapes off grains of pollen from its anthers. Next, she flies to a flower that is a bit more mature to lay her eggs at the base of the ovary. She marks the spot using a special scent so that other females know she laid eggs there.

She then deposits the pollen on the stigma tip, ensuring it will be pollinated and then produce a fruit containing seeds. The hatched yucca moth caterpillars will munch on the fruit and grow until they are large enough to turn into a pupa.

One of these yucca moths may have laid her eggs in this yucca flower.

AFTER THE BLOOM

What happens after a flower withers? Does it become something else? Be a flower investigator and discover what happens.

MATERIALS

- 10 large twist ties
- Marker with waterproof ink
- Plant journal
- Pen or pencil
- Magnifying glass
- Colored pencils or markers (optional)
- Camera (optional)

1. Get permission to investigate a garden with blossoms, such as a flower or vegetable garden, or a weed patch.

2. Number the twist ties 1 through 10, using a marker with waterproof ink.

3. Attach a tie around the stem below each blossom on a variety of flowers.

4. In your plant journal, take notes about each type of flower a tie is attached to. Record the condition of the flower, for example, "fresh" or "starting to wither." And don't forget to write the date.

5. In one week, check on the flowers. Examine them with the magnifying glass, and then write descriptions in your journal. Optional: Sketch or photograph the flowers. Later you can add prints of your photos to your journal.

6. Continue to check each flower for three more weeks and describe any changes you notice.

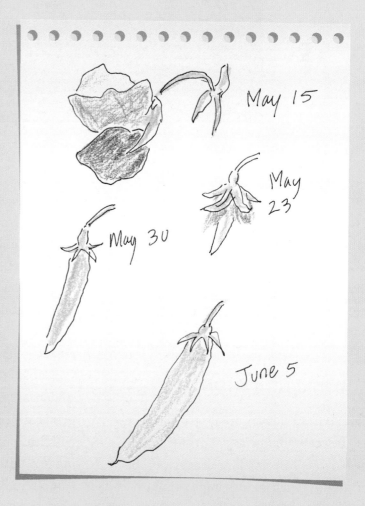

Can you find the crab spider?

When the moths emerge from their pupa the following spring, they will mate, and the females will repeat the same process as their mother did. The yucca moth is the only pollinator of the yucca, and yucca is the moth's only food plant. Neither would survive without this close relationship, which has occurred for millions of years.

Beware of Traps

Though most flowers are pretty, they can also be pretty dangerous. Lurking amid the blossoms are small creatures looking for prey. As their names imply, ambush bugs, assassin bugs, and robber flies are not creatures that peaceful pollinators want to meet. Each of these hunting insects has stout front legs for holding onto prey, piercing mouthparts for drinking blood, and camouflage to disguise themselves as they lie in wait. Once they snag a pollinator, they inject digestive juices that liquefy the insides of their prey and then drink their meal.

Named for their crab-like shape, crab spiders are often the same color as a flower's petals. Able to sit still for hours, they wait with legs outstretched until an unsuspecting bee, butterfly, or fly comes within reach. A moth or bee sitting motionless on a flower could turn out to be a victim of this patient spider.

Flower Climbing Gyms

A close inspection of a flower reveals a world of tiny visitors that don't play a part in reproduction, such as thrips, mites, and ants. They crawl about eating pollen, flower parts, and nectar. For example, even though ants feed on pollen and nectar, they rarely pollinate flowers because they don't consistently visit one flower after another of the same species like a butterfly or bee does. Thrips, recognized by their feathery wings and tubelike heads, eat the parts of old flowers. Florists dislike thrips because they want cut flowers to look fresh. Thrips can be found by shaking an aging blossom over a piece of paper. Tiny mites also inhabit blossoms, and males have been seen hitchhiking from one flower to another in the nostrils of hummingbirds as they seek females to mate with.

Sunflower Sun Trackers

It has long been known that sunflowers turn during the day to face the sun. As they mature they primarily turn to face the sun in the morning when temperatures are cool. Five times as many pollinators visit these warmer blossoms than cooler ones, which is no surprise since bees and other pollinators need warm temperatures to move around.

Petalless Flowers

Not all flowers are showy. Wind-pollinated flowers, such as those found on curly dock, meadow rue, sedges, and grasses, have no need to attract pollinators, so they lack petals.

Marsh marigold, waterfall buttercup, miterwort, and buckwheat flowers look like they have petals, but they have petal-like sepals instead. Unlike triangular green sepals of strawberry or tomato flowers, the white sepals of waterfall buttercups catch the eye, while the minute green petals go unnoticed at the base of the stamens and pistils. Buckwheat and marsh marigold flowers also have petal-like sepals rather than petals. In addition to acting as covers for buds and developing fruits, the sepals in these flowers attract pollinators.

The sepals on a columbine flower look like typical triangular petals, while the true petals are long tubes with nectar bulbs at the tip. Sphinx moths and hummingbirds have tongues that are long enough to reach the end of the tubes.

Tricky Orchids

The South American bucket orchid (*Coryanthes*) uses drunk bees in its reproductive process. It attracts male euglossine bees with a scent that seems to intoxicate the bees. In this drunken condition the bees slip on the smooth petal surface of the orchid and slide down into the bucket-like structure that gives the orchid its name. The only escape is through a narrow passage where the bee picks up a packet of pollen that sticks to its body. It then carries the pollen to the next blossom.

6

Fabulous Fruit

What if someone told you that tomatoes, pea pods, corn kernels, and pumpkins were all fruits? You might not believe them! Many people think of these foods as vegetables. As a budding plantologist (botanist), you can now learn the truth about fruit. Botanically speaking, all fruits are simply the swollen female part of the flower, the ovary. Bananas, pumpkins, tomatoes, blueberries, and almonds are all actually fruits!

A zucchini squash is a fruit. Note the shriveled petals on its tip.

Picture bee after bee delivering pollen to the stigma on a female pumpkin flower as they feed on nectar. Like other squash plants, pumpkins have flowers that have either only stamens (and are thus male) or only pistils (and are therefore female). The pollen fertilizes the ovules (eggs) in the flower's ovary. The ovary, which is about the size of a pencil tip, soon begins to swell as seeds develop inside. The ovary grows each day, enlarging and swelling. Before long it is 10 times its original size and resembles a pumpkin. It grows and grows until it is 100 times its original size and then 1,000 times. If it is a champion pumpkin, it may reach 10,000 or more times its original size.

Inside are numerous seeds, each composed of the embryo wrapped in a seed coat. These are enclosed in the swollen ovary wall, also known as the **pericarp**. On the outside is a thick skin, also called an **exocarp**. In the pumpkin, which is actually a large berry, the innermost part (called the pithy endocarp) is laced with slimy fibers surrounding pockets filled with seeds. Surrounding the endocarp is the fleshy part of the fruit known as the **mesocarp**. This is what is used to make pumpkin pie!

BIG FRUIT, LITTLE FRUIT

Some varieties of squashes can grow very large under the right conditions. A 1,689-pound (766 kilogram) pumpkin grown in Rhode Island in 2007 was shown at the Topsfield Fair in Massachusetts. Melons are another member of the squash family. A watermelon grown in Hope, Arkansas, in 2006 may be the world champion. At 268.8 pounds (121 kilograms), it broke the previous record of a watermelon grown by the same farmer in 1985, which weighed 260 pounds (118 kilograms). The smallest fruit is that of duckweed, which is about the size of a salt grain. It is classified as a utricle, a dry fruit whose single seed is enclosed in a balloon-like ovary wall.

Catalog of Fruit Types

Just like there are many types of homes, such as tents, trailers, cottages, and mansions, there are also many types of fruit. Impress your family and friends by using the botanical names of the fruits we eat.

🍃 **Simple one-seeded fruits:** Some fruits don't seem like fruits at all. In fact, most people call simple fruits a seed. For example, a corn kernel is often referred to as a seed, as are other grains such as barley, wheat, rice, and oats. Each of these is actually a one-seeded fruit called a caryopsis, which is made up of an ovary wall fused to the seed coat inside. Next time you go to the movie theater, think about those delicious popped caryopses you'll be gobbling during the film.

An achene is another type of simple fruit in plants in the sunflower, buckwheat, and buttercup families. Within an achene the seed is loosely attached to the ovary wall, just like a sunflower seed inside its "shell."

🍃 **Nuts, it's a fruit:** Even nuts are fruits. Each nut, whether it is a hazelnut from a hazel shrub or an acorn from a shrub oak, is a one-seeded fruit with a hard shell.

🍃 **Crunchy fruit:** Another type of fruit is the dry multiseeded capsule in poppies, irises, and mallows (such as cotton). This type of fruit is made up of sections of an ovary called carpels that each contain ovules. Each carpel will develop seeds, and the seed capsule often splits between the carpel walls.

🍃 **Berry strange:** Picture a juicy berry. Do you picture a tomato, grape, kiwifruit, cucumber, or blueberry? According to botanists, a fleshy fruit formed from the ripened ovary wall of a single flower with one seed or more inside the flesh is defined as a berry. By this definition tomatoes, grapes, kiwifruit, and cucumbers *are* considered berries. Currants, avocados, eggplants, peppers, watermelons, and pomegranates fit within this category, too, and are classified as berries. It may be hard to think of a watermelon or cucumber as a berry. That

Corn kernels are a type of one-seeded fruit known as a caryopsis. *CSIRO*

This iris seed capsule is considered a dry fruit.

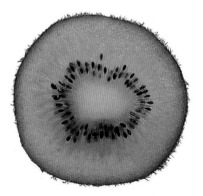

A kiwifruit is a berry with seeds in the center and a fleshy swollen ovary wall.

WHO EATS WHAT

When bush branches are laden with fruit, the neighborhood becomes noisier with the sounds of hungry birds hastily picking berries or pecking larger fruits. Find out who the fruit looters are in your neighborhood by setting up a spy station.

MATERIALS

- Lawn chair
- Binoculars
- Bird field guide
- Plant journal
- Pen or pencil

1. Set up your chair 15 to 20 feet (5 to 6 meters) from a shrub with ripe fruit.

2. Spy on any birds that are eating and use the bird field guide to identify them.

3. Write down the date and time you saw each bird in your plant journal. Record how many total birds you see at one time. Note how many birds of each species you see.

4. Check the same spot the next day. Is the bush still busy with birds at the same time?

you ever eaten the pithy layer underneath an orange or grapefruit peel? It has a bitter flavor due to the presence of a chemical called limonin. Some folks don't mind the bitter flavor of the pith, but most avoid eating it.

Un-berries

Just as butterflies and dragonflies are not true flies, some berries are not technically berries. Not all fruits with *berry* in their names are berries.

- **Strawberries:** Have you ever noticed that the outside of a strawberry has tiny seeds embedded in the red flesh? If a berry has seeds enclosed within the fleshy ripe ovary, what do we call a strawberry? A strawberry flower has many pistils embedded in a small mound called a receptacle. Once the ovules are fertilized, the ovaries of each of the many pistils become a simple fruit known as an achene. Meanwhile, the receptacle grows and becomes sweet and fleshy with the achenes embedded, like sprinkles, on its surface. Since the receptacle is not part of the ovary, a strawberry is regarded as an accessory fruit.

is why botanists classify berries with tough, thick rinds as pepos. Pumpkins and other squashes are also pepos.

A hesperidium is another category of berry. This term is used for fruits in the citrus family, which have a leathery rind containing oil glands in small pits. The strong fragrance we smell when

removing the peel of a lemon or orange comes from these glands. Underneath the skin (peel) are the juicy sections, each a carpel, with the familiar fluid-filled sacs. As you bite into a section of an orange, consider that these sacs filled with refreshing juice are actually hair cells that no longer resemble hair. Have

A strawberry is not a real berry. *Shutterstock*

By now you may be thinking botanists just make plants more complicated, but it is plants that are complex. Precise, specialized language is needed to explain this complexity. So, all along we have been calling that delicious red fruit a berry when it is actually an accessory fruit. That doesn't mean that now you should call it a "straw accessory fruit." The fact that a strawberry is an accessory fruit explains why it doesn't look like a blueberry. And no matter what it is called, a strawberry still tastes good.

- **Pineapples:** A pineapple is an accessory fruit similar in structure to a strawberry but much larger. Oddly, a pineapple doesn't grow on a pine tree or taste like an apple. Centuries ago, the English thought this sweet fruit looked like a pine cone and started calling it a pineapple. Other accessory fruits include figs and mulberries.

- **Pome:** A hawthorn shrub has a fruit, sometimes called a haw, that looks like a berry. Like berries, it has seeds surrounded by flesh. Like accessory fruits, the fleshy part of a pome is not from the ovary but from another a part of the flower called a hypanthium. This cuplike structure, made up of part of the sepals and petals, swells to become the fleshy part of the haw.

- **Clumped fruit:** If you carefully inspect a raspberry or blackberry, you'll see that it is composed of many little berrylike sections, each with a seed inside, that are clumped together to make one fruit. Unlike a simple berry, such as a blueberry, which develops from one ovary, these berries are made from merging the ovaries of many pistils that were separate within one flower. Each little part is like a miniature berry, so instead of being called a berry, a raspberry is referred to as an aggregate fruit.

- **Pitted fruit:** Don't be duped by a drupe! Fruits like a chokecherry, a holly, or a poison oak "berry" with one or more hard pits inside are called drupes. They are not berries because the pit is part of the ovary as well as the fleshy part surrounding it. Inside the pit is the actual seed.

Going Bananas

Not only do bananas not grow on trees, because a banana plant is not a tree, but bananas are also considered berries. The modern banana doesn't look like a berry, and the main cultivars, those on plantations, are mostly seedless. The few seeds

A blackberry is made up of many small berries clumped together.

that may exist are shrunk to tiny black specks along the central line inside a split banana.

The bananas we buy at the store originated from a wild plant known as *Musa acuminata* that grows in Southeast Asia. Looking at the fruits of the wild banana, it's not hard to see that they are berries.

Before they were cultivated 8,000 years ago and bred to create larger fruits, there were as many as 160 bananas in each bunch. Each banana was only a bit larger than a person's thumb. Like a true berry, inside the fleshy fruit were 15–60 seeds, each slightly smaller in diameter than the size of a popcorn kernel. Instead of being able to bite off a large mouthful and quickly chew it before swallowing, each little bite of these mini bananas would require spitting out seeds, just like when eating a slice of seeded watermelon.

Travel Deals

Plants with fruits offer both the plants and animals a special deal. Animals eat the fruits and then transport their seeds away from the parent plant, often to a better site to grow.

- **Bird express:** A robin eats a blackberry and then flies through a grove of trees. Meanwhile, it is digesting the berry, and the kayak-shaped blackberry seeds glide through its digestive system. After 30 minutes the robin perches on a limb to sing or preen its feathers. The seeds travel rapidly through the robin's digestive tract and are expelled in its droppings as it takes off in flight. The seeds fall to the forest floor and, accompanied by fertilizer, are ready to grow when the right conditions exist.

  Birds often perch on telephone lines or fences, where berry plants soon sprout. Migrating birds moving north or south may transport seeds for many

TRY THIS!

ACCESSORY-FRUIT SALAD

Slice, dice, mix! Enjoy a sweet accessory-fruit salad with family or friends.

ADULT SUPERVISION REQUIRED

INGREDIENTS

- 2 pints of strawberries
- 1 cup fresh or dried figs
- 1 ripe pineapple

MATERIALS

- Colander
- Cutting board
- Knife
- Medium-sized mixing bowl
- 2 large spoons

1. Place the strawberries and fresh figs in the colander and rinse them with clean water.

2. With adult supervision, place the pineapple on the cutting board and use a knife to trim off the skin.

3. Remove the green sepals (the "caps") from the strawberries.

4. Cut the fruits into pieces and place them together in the mixing bowl.

5. Toss with the spoons and serve!

miles. Birds are the ideal seed dispersers because of their ability to carry seeds long distances. Many species of birds can transport seeds in their digestive tracts more than 100 miles (161 kilometers) and are responsible for bringing new plant species to islands. The new plants on newly formed volcanic islands far out in the ocean come from seeds deposited in the droppings of killdeer and stints. These two species of shore birds sometimes eat fruits, such as hackberries, during long migrations. The birds can hold seeds in their guts for a week or more, long enough for the seeds to be carried thousands of miles.

Exclusive meals: Mammals and reptiles also eat fruits and may transport seeds, but sometimes the seeds are crushed while being eaten. Since birds can carry seeds farther, many fruits that are edible to birds are distasteful or poisonous to mammals. Birds can eat pokeberries, baneberries, and deadly nightshade berries, fruits that most mammals leave alone.

Bear delivery service: Certain fruits are distributed by both birds and mammals, particularly bears. In autumn, large bear droppings full of partially

TRY THIS!

BERRY SHAKE

Wash, peel, measure, blend! Have a berry nice party with your berry best friends as you make this delicious fruit shake. (Serves 4)

ADULT SUPERVISION REQUIRED

INGREDIENTS

- 1 cup blueberries (fresh or frozen)
- 2 ripe bananas
- 2 cups plain yogurt (low fat or nonfat)
- 1 tablespoon honey or maple syrup

MATERIALS

- Colander
- Blender
- 4 tall glasses

1. Place the blueberries in the colander and rinse them.

2. Peel the bananas and place them in the blender.

3. Add the yogurt, blueberries, and sweetener to the blender.

4. Blend until smooth and serve in the glasses.

A stint, one of the best long-distance seed carriers.

digested manzanita berries are a common sight in California oak woodlands. Deer mice collect and bury intact seeds to eat later in winter. These scavenged seeds are more likely to germinate and produce a new shrub than those that remain in the bear scat (poop). Black bears eat may other types of berries and can chow down on more than 30,000 berries in a single day!

🍃 **Spitting up:** Large birds are important dispersers of large seeds in tropical forests. The great hornbill, a large-billed Asian bird, is nicknamed the "farmer of the forest" for its role in delivering seeds to suitable growing sites. After eating a fruit, a hornbill regurgitates, throws up, the seeds. In one forest in India they were observed eating at least 80 species of fruits. The resplendent quetzal eats wild avocados and other large-seeded tropical fruits in Central America. Like the hornbill, it regurgitates the seeds in areas far away from the parent plant and regenerates the forest.

Beware Berries

Anyone who has tasted a wild blueberry or strawberry will want to discover more wild fruits in forests and fields. However, not all wild fruit belongs in our mouths. Each year thousands of children become severely ill from eating poisonous fruit. Here is a list of common poison fruits to keep away from.

🍃 **Pokeberry:** These juicy black and purple berries are prized snacks for cardinals, mockingbirds, and gray catbirds. But unless you are also a bird, leave them alone. If you eat them, you might have to make a wild dash to the bathroom to vomit and deal with diarrhea. Worse yet, you may end up visiting the hospital.

🍃 **Deadly nightshade:** The toxin from deadly nightshade was used to make

(*left*) Some birds, like quetzals, regurgitate seeds that are too large to pass through their digestive tract.

(*right*) These unripe pokeberries grow where the ground has been disturbed.

poison arrows. It is so deadly that eating just two to five berries can lead to death.

🍃 **Jerusalem cherry:** This houseplant also belongs to the nightshade family. Eating the berries of this plant causes symptoms similar to eating pokeberries, and in extreme cases can cause paralysis.

🍃 **Holly berry:** Those cheerful sprigs of shiny leaves and colorful red berries that decorate homes during Christmas can ruin any holiday if they are ingested. Eating holly berries will eliminate holiday cheer as you'll spend your time rushing to the bathroom.

🍃 **Ivy berry:** The berries on leafy ivy plants climbing over fences, around tree trunks, or up a chimney may look edible, but ingesting them is not a pleasant experience. Not only are they bitter, but the sharp needlelike crystals in the berry also cause pain and swelling in the lips, tongue, and skin of anyone who eats them.

🍃 **Privet berry:** Privet hedges provide privacy. Purple splotches on your sidewalk or the family car are signs that birds enjoy their berries, but don't be tempted to try one yourself. Eating just one or two will cause nausea, abdominal pain,

vomiting, and diarrhea. Eating more than that can be fatal.

🍃 **Asparagus fruit:** After asparagus shoots emerge, they send up flowering stems that produce red berries that look good to eat. But like other poisonous berries, eating them will ruin your day as you purge your digestive system.

Water Berry

It's a brutally hot day in the Kalahari Desert thousands of years ago, and water is scarce. Growing in the sandy soil is a small, round melon berry the size of a chicken egg. The skin is hard and needs to be opened with a sharp object like a rock. The fruit inside is moist and packed with seeds. It looks tasty, but the fruit is bitter, and so are the seeds. Despite the bitter flavor, the seeds are nutty and nutritious. Eating too many of the seeds or too much of the bitter fruit, however, can cause a stomachache. Perhaps this berry could be called a bitter water berry.

A thousand years later in Egypt, farmers grow a plant that looks something like the bitter water berry, but it is larger and oblong. They grow and store it for the dry season, when it is used as a source of water.

Over hundreds of years, farmers plant only the seeds of the water berries that are

both less bitter and larger. By AD 200, these berries are no longer bitter and no longer small. Selective breeding produced sweeter fruits, with red flesh; the color associated with the higher sugar content is red.

This is how the modern watermelon was born. It has become larger and sweeter over 5,000 years. After these many years of selective breeding, it changed from a bitter yellow-fleshed berry to the 10- to 20-pound (5- to 9-kilogram) melons that are a sweet, juicy treat on a hot summer day.

Selective Plant Breeding

All of our agricultural crops that find their way to the supermarket produce section or to farmer's markets came from wild plants that grew long ago. The natural descendants of those wild ancestors still grow naturally in wild landscapes from bogs to deserts, forests to fields. Some, like the wild strawberry, are easy to recognize as a relative of the cultivated ones. Like many plants, the cultivated strawberry was bred to be larger and more productive. Though not the case with watermelons, one cost of breeding a bigger and more prolific fruit is that they are not as tasty as the wild fruit. Folks who get the chance to taste a ripe wild strawberry may end up preferring its

TOMATO TASTE TEST

Shop, pick, slice, serve! Invite friends and family to participate in a blind taste test to determine their favorite tomato varieties.

ADULT SUPERVISION REQUIRED

MATERIALS

- 4 varieties of tomatoes, gathered from a local garden (maybe yours) or bought from a farmer's market, farm stand, or grocery store
- Colander
- Knife
- Cutting board
- 4 plates
- 4 sticky notes, labeled 1, 2, 3, and 4
- 4 friends or volunteer taste-testers
- 4 bandanas
- Toothpicks
- 4 glasses and a pitcher of water or lemonade
- Pen or pencil
- Plant journal

1. Place the tomatoes in the colander and rinse them.

2. With adult supervision, slice the tomatoes into bite-sized pieces on the cutting board.

3. Place the slices of each type of tomato on a separate plate.

4. Label the plates 1 through 4 with the sticky notes.

5. Blindfold each volunteer with a bandana.

6. Serve each volunteer a tomato sample on a toothpick from plate #1.

7. Give the volunteers a drink to clear their tastebuds.

8. Repeat for each of the four tomato varieties.

9. At the end of the test, before removing their blindfolds, ask the volunteers which sample was their favorite and what they liked best about it.

10. Record the results in your plant journal.

flavor to the mammoth modern strawberry. Some fruits, like modern tomatoes, have been selectively bred for characteristics other than flavor, such as the ability to be shipped long distances without damage and to be harvested when still green.

The Circle of Life

Fruits contain seeds, the packages of future plant life. Plants such as tomatoes grow for just one season. In that season they start from a seed, grow into a seedling, and finally become a mature plant that produces flowers that change into fruits after pollination. The fruit seeds fall or are carried to a new spot to grow. Other plants, such as a currant bush, may grow for many years. Each year it produces berries that provide seeds for future currant shrubs.

The future shrubs might grow nearby, or the seeds might be carried long distances by birds to perhaps grow where currants have never grown before.

Wild strawberries are small and tasty.

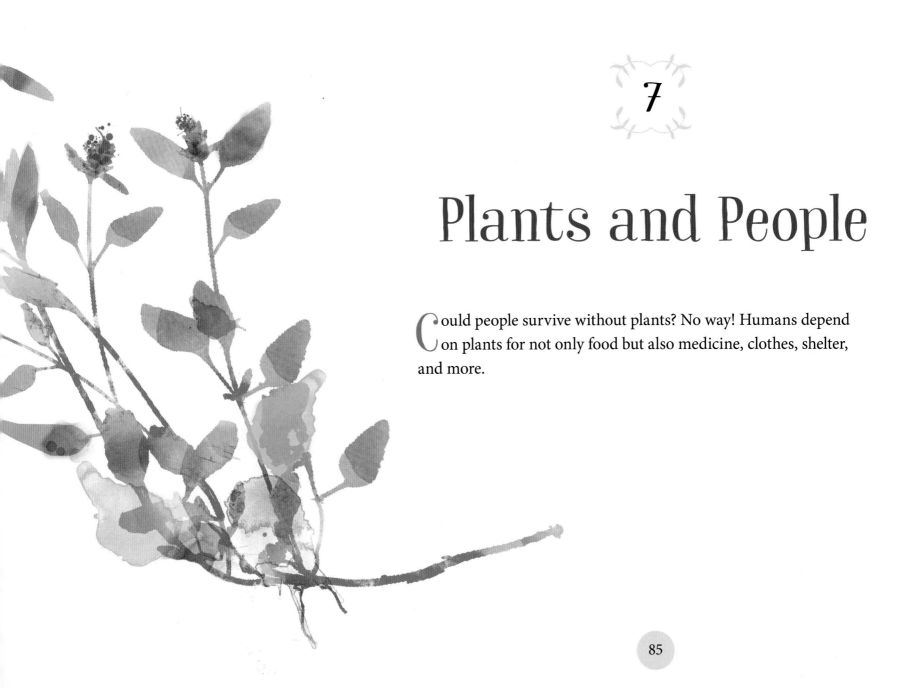

7

Plants and People

Could people survive without plants? No way! Humans depend on plants for not only food but also medicine, clothes, shelter, and more.

Take Two Leaves and Rest

Today the advice for a health problem perhaps might be, "Take two pills and rest." But what is inside the pills can be a mystery. Hundreds of years ago, pills were not yet invented, and most remedies came from plants. In many parts of the world, they still do.

Bugle is a common mint related to bugleweed in Kenya.

Within the past couple of centuries, drugs derived from chemicals in plants have been developed for specific health problems. For example, digoxin, a drug used to treat heart failure, is based on a substance found in foxglove, or digitalis, a common garden flower. The decongestant pseudoephedrine is a human-made chemical identical to natural substances in species such as the ephedra plant.

Scientists are always searching for plants that might help treat diseases with no known cures. A species of common mint growing in East Africa called bugleweed, *Ajuga remota*, has been used by traditional Kenyan herbalists to treat malaria. Medical researchers hope it may be the source of a new antimalarial drug. A common species of *Ajuga*, called bugle, grows in Europe and is used as a ground cover in gardens in North America. Its leaves are used to stop internal bleeding.

Sweet and Natural Smelling

Some plants have a foul aroma, but many others have pleasant scents that humans use in everything from soaps to toothpaste. The fresh outdoor smell of plant fragrances makes them popular for all sorts of body products. Think of some products we use every day:

- Spearmint- or berry-flavored toothpastes
- Lotions, creams, and soaps scented with lavender, basil, rose, or strawberry
- Shampoos scented with lemon verbena or honeysuckle
- Soaps, salves, body oils, creams, and cosmetics made from lavender oil

Grow Some Nice Threads

Are you wearing a plant? Check the labels inside your clothes before you answer. If the labels include any of the plant fibers in the following list, you are wearing clothing made from the fibers of a plant.

- **Cotton:** Jeans, sweats, T-shirts, undies, hoodies, and socks may be made with threads from cotton fibers. These long strands grow around cottonseeds, and if left unharvested they will carry the seeds off in the breeze like the fluff attached to a dandelion seed. Years ago, thousands of miles away from each other, ancient peoples in central Mexico and the Indian subcontinent discovered how to make cloth from cottonseed

After cotton flowers are pollinated, they transform into cotton bolls full of fibers.

fibers. Soon they began to domesticate the cotton plants and breed them to develop plants that produce more and longer seed fibers. Today cotton is the most used of all plant fibers. Sheets, towels, bandages, clothing, drapes, and furniture upholstery are made from cotton. Rags from old cotton cloth are used to make fine paper and insulation.

🍃 **Linen:** A field of blooming flax flowers is beautiful. This was a common sight throughout Europe, the Middle East, and Asia for thousands of years. Flax was first cultivated in the Middle East more than 9,000 years ago. Four thousand years later, flax was being grown in Europe, China, and India. Fibers from stems of flax plants are used to make a fine fabric called linen, which was worn by priests in ancient Egypt and used to make sails for Roman ships. Today fine suits, dresses, tablecloths, and napkins are made of linen. Paper money is 75 percent cotton and

WHAT'S THAT PLANT, DOC?

Many of the first botanists were trained as physicians because they had been schooled in using plants as remedies. A doctor's case contained plant medicines for a variety of health problems.

🍃 **Arnica:** Used to treat aching muscles and nasty bruises.
🍃 **Yarrow:** Good for treating fever, diarrhea, loss of appetite, and intestinal or menstrual cramping, and to relieve toothache pain.
🍃 **Turmeric:** Used in India and elsewhere for relieving joint pain, stomachaches, and heartburn, and for healing wounds.
🍃 **Chamomile:** Settles upset stomachs and calms tense nerves.
🍃 **Parsley:** Treats bad breath.
🍃 **Aloe vera:** Helps heal minor burns.

Chamomile grows in both gardens and fields.

WONDER GRASS

Picture a grass that has a woody stem and grows as tall as a nine-story building. There are over 1,000 species of this grass on the planet. Some grow barely 10 feet (3 meters) tall with a stem as thick as a broom handle, while other species grow taller than a giraffe with a stem thicker than a baseball bat. You may have guessed that this wonder grass is bamboo, and humans use it in a variety of ways.

Chopsticks, ladles, and food containers are fashioned from bamboo stalks. A home can even be built out of bamboo stalks, with a bamboo floor, bamboo furniture, and a bamboo fence around it. The inhabitants could dress in clothes made from bamboo fabric and wear a bamboo helmet while riding a bamboo bike or skateboard. Bamboo is less likely to break under pressure or tension than wood, brick, concrete, or steel. It's so sturdy that bamboo scaffolds many stories high are assembled during the construction of tall buildings. Since it grows rapidly, new bamboo for making all these products is available faster than other materials from natural sources.

People ride bamboo bikes in Argentina and many other countries.

25 percent linen. Flax fibers are also used in making paper. More than twice as strong as cotton fibers, flax fibers are better for making strong canvas sailcloth, tarps, artists' canvases, and durable clothing.

Hemp: Pure hemp fabric feels like linen. Hemp fibers have long been used to make canvas. In fact, the word *canvas* is derived from *cannabis*, the Romans' name for hemp. Paper from hemp does not yellow like paper made from wood pulp does. Thomas Jefferson wrote his first two drafts of the Declaration of Independence on hemp paper. Today bibles, coffee filters, and even money are made out of hemp paper. More than 100,000 tons of hemp fibers were needed to make the sails and rope rigging for the USS *Constitution*, also known as "Old Ironsides." During World War II the US government's "Hemp for Victory" campaign encouraged farmers to grow more hemp because the war effort required a large amount of fiber. Hemp fabric is a good choice for sturdy clothing as well as stylish fashions. In 2016 an eco-friendly car, the Kestrel, was manufactured in Canada. It had a body composed of hemp fibers estimated to be at least 10 times more dent-resistant than steel!

🍃 **Jute:** Grown for centuries in Africa and Asia, jute is the second largest fiber crop after cotton. Jute stems, like those of flax and hemp, are the source of fibers used in everything from ropes to rugs and from paper to panels for airplanes. Sacks of Hessian cloth, a fabric made from jute, are used to transport coffee beans, tea, and tobacco, as well as to make sandbags to ward off floodwaters.

🍃 **Sisal:** If you play a game of darts with a high-quality target, chances are it is made with sisal fibers. Some expensive cowboy hats are also made of sisal. Sisal is also used to make custom floor

Sacks made of jute are used to ship coffee beans.

FIBER FINDS

Inspect, compare, and display! As you examine fabrics you'll understand why they vary in texture.

MATERIALS

🌱 Magnifying glass (to read labels more easily)

🌱 Pen or pencil

🌱 Plant journal

1. Rummage through your closet and dresser and read the labels of your clothing to discover the source of the fibers. Polyester, nylon, spandex, Lycra, and acrylic are all synthetic or chemically produced fibers.

2. Compare the qualities, such as smoothness, flexibility, and durability, of the fabrics. Do you notice a difference between synthetic material such as polyester or Lycra and natural plant fibers such as cotton or flax?

3. Find a few more pieces of clothing. Before looking at the labels, try to identify the fabric by just touching or looking at it. Display the clothing for friends and family and test their fabric identification skills.

4. Record your favorite plant-based fabrics in your plant journal and bring it along the next time you shop for clothes.

In this 15th-century tapestry, *The Hunt of the Unicorn*, the yellow color comes from the woad plant and the red from the madder plant.

manufacture not only hats, mats, and dartboards but also footwear, carpets, and bags.

- **Milkweed and dogbane:** These plants are also sources of fibers. Orioles and other birds collect strands from old plant stalks to weave their intricate socklike nests.

Growing Colors: Plant Dyes

During most of humankind's existence, the dyes used to color textiles made from cotton, flax, and other plant fibers also came from plants. It was fairly easy to find plants to produce green, yellow, and brown dyes. Plants that yielded the colors blue and red were more difficult to come by.

- Around 4,000 years ago, people in India discovered how to get a red color from the roots of the madder plant.

- More than 2,000 years ago, Egyptians made a dye from woad leaves to give fabrics a blue color. This member of the mustard family grows so easily it is sometimes considered a weed. As far back as 6,000 years ago, ancient Peruvians discovered they could use the indigo plant to make a blue dye. Like

mats for luxury cars. All of these items are made from fibers grown mostly in Brazil or Africa. Unlike flax, jute, or hemp fibers, which are from stems, sisal fibers come from the plant's tough spear-like leaves. After harvesting, these leaves are crushed, beaten, and brushed to separate the strong strands used to

many other plants in the pea family, indigo fertilizes the soil, so it can grow where other crops have depleted soils. Native to central Asia and the Caucuses, indigo now grows without cultivation in many parts of Africa and Asia. In Medieval times cities became wealthy from producing textile dyes from madder and indigo.

🍃 To prevent natural dyes from washing out or fading, a mordant or dye fixative is used. Derived from the Latin word *mordere*, meaning "to bite," a mordant makes a dye "hold fast" as if it is biting the fabric. Natural mordants are tannin, from oak galls, and fermented urine. The color of the dye will vary depending on the type of mordant used.

🍃 Lichens yield a wide range of colors, as do parts of common garden plants such as onion skins and coreopsis flowers (gold), and carrot tops and yarrow leaves (green).

Green Cleanup Crew

Besides feeding, clothing, and providing shelter for people, plants help humanity in other ways. Toxic waste produced by mines, factories, or power plants is hazardous to our health and that of other organisms. It needs to be disposed of in a special place where it can't contaminate the water, air, or soil.

When waste is dumped in a field, the soil becomes contaminated, endangering the health of anyone living nearby. Cleaning up the mess is very expensive because truckloads of soil must be excavated and transported to a safe disposal site. Across the world toxic waste sites are polluting local environments due to lack of money to clean them up.

Botanists have learned that some plants are naturally good cleansers of toxic substances. For example, geraniums, Mexican sunflowers, heartleaf hempvine, and goatweed remove toxins from earth. When they die in autumn, the plants can be harvested and burned at safe disposal sites. The toxic ash takes up just a fraction of the space of mountains of poisonous soil. And the cost is also just a fraction of that for hauling away dirt, although total removal takes longer. Removal of toxins by plants is slower, taking year after year until the site is safe.

Geraniums help remove toxins from soil.

This plant work quietly improves the landscape. Imagine bright-red geraniums and pretty yellow sunflowers blooming inside a chain-link fence with Stay Out, Toxic Waste signs.

Plants like Mexican sunflowers, heartleaf hemp vine, and goatweed that are considered nasty weeds on farms can be valuable partners in cleaning up our environment. Botanists call this cleanup method phytoremediation. *Phyto* means "from plants" and *remediation* refers to a remedy or fix.

Nature's Wastewater Treatment

Who wants to swim in water full of raw sewage? Unfortunately, in some places sewage is still dumped into oceans, lakes, and rivers. When this occurs, the water becomes unfit to drink, water crops, or swim in. Contaminated fish and shellfish are no longer safe to eat. Disposing of sewage safely is costly, but plant **ecologists** are discovering more affordable ways to treat sewage with the help of plants.

- Natural wetlands, such as fresh and saltwater marshes, naturally filter toxins and nutrients from the water. Artificial wetlands can be grown with cattails and bulrushes to provide the same filtering functions.

- Both rooted and floating plants physically trap particles in wastewater containing pollutants. The roots also provide homes for useful bacteria.

- Just as in phytoremediation, nutrients and toxic substances are sucked up by roots and stored in plant parts.

- Microorganisms such as soil bacteria extract energy from solid compounds, such as carbon. They then convert the solids to gases. Some bacteria convert nitrogen solids to ammonium gas. Others change ammonia into nitrate that cattails and bulrush absorb through their roots, stimulating their growth.

- Artificial wetlands have been established to help process wastewater throughout the world, from California to Florida to India, Thailand, the Philippines, and France. These "living" sewage treatment facilities cost less than other facilities. They also provide a habitat for wildlife in areas where wetlands have been destroyed. In Arcata, California, the wastewater marsh is like a park with trails for walking and biking, and lots of ducks and other birds to watch.

Native Wisdom: Sustaining Ecosystems

"If we use a plant respectfully, it will stay with us, and flourish." —Lena, a Mohawk elder

For years Native Americans such as the Pomo, Ojibwa, and Miwok have been described as hunter-gatherers. This label might imply that they don't have much control over their food sources. In reality, they are master managers of natural landscapes. Botanists may label plants such as blue elderberry and sweetgrass as wild plants, but where these plants grow on Native American ancestral lands they may be considered as cultivated, like a field of pumpkins or corn. Instead of plowing the earth and planting seeds, indigenous people use fire and special harvesting techniques. These practices stimulate the growth of plants to increase the amount and improve the quality of both food and harvestable materials.

- Blue elderberry has pithy stems that are easy to hollow out. The stems with the longest space between nodes, where leaf stems arise, are the best for making flutes and a rhythm instrument called a clapper stick. Miwok flute makers know that burning an elderberry shrub causes it to send up shoots with long, straight stems. The ash-burned stem is so rich in nutrients it acts as a fertilizer to help the elderberry bush regrow rapidly. The Miwok use fire in the same way to produce straight, long stems on spicebush, which are used to make arrow shafts, and on sourberry shrubs, used to make baskets.

- Pomo women harvest both edible and useful bulbs from many plants. Their harvesting method makes the remaining bulbs grow more strongly and thus produce more bulbs. Plants such as wild onion, mariposa lily, and soap plant are more abundant in patches where bulbs are harvested. Fire also favors the growth of bulbs.

- Sweetgrass grows across the northern part of the world. It is used for medicine and basket making, and is burned ceremonially. In national parks and other preserves, many managers believe wild places need to be left alone for plants to thrive. Others understand that natural processes like fire and flood renew wild **ecosystems**, but most consider traditional harvesting to be harmful to "wild plants." Studies of traditional harvesting

Soap plant's stiff fibers and sticky bulb can be used to make a strong brush.

of sweetgrass show that harvested sites are healthier than those left alone. According to elder basket makers, there are basic rules and rituals regarding harvesting: "Leave a gift [like tobacco leaves]. Ask permission to harvest, and never take more than half."

Fortunately, as many land managers learn more about indigenous plants, they accept native wisdom, which teaches people to respect plants and see people as a part of nature.

The Future of Food: Deciding How We Grow Our Meals

Imagine a field with tall cornstalks, twining beans, sprawling squash plants, and peppers. A jay flies by, squawking, "Pedro, Pedro, Pedro." This scene has existed in places like Mexico for centuries, where people have been cultivating corn (also known as maize) on small family plots called milpas.

In each region, the variety of corn is specially suited to the soils and climate. In the subtropical Yucatan, towering corn plants rise out of rocky limestone fields that depend on rain. In the high mountains of central Mexico, the corn thrives in rich soils with almost daily rainfall and frosty nights. Year after year the farmers, known as campesinos, put aside some of the kernels for planting the next season.

Now picture vast cornfields in a place like Iowa, where large amounts of fertilizer, **pesticides**, and **herbicides** are used to ensure high production. Farmers there have to purchase seeds for genetically modified

(GMO) corn that is not damaged by a large amount of herbicides. Each year they must buy more **hybrid** or GMO seeds. GMO corn produces only sterile seeds, ones that are not able to grow into corn plants.

Unlike the campesinos, most Iowan farmers must spend so much money to grow their crops that they ask for funds from the government. This type of farming produces large harvests of corn that is neither flavorful nor as nutritious as the old varieties of corn. Much of it is used to feed livestock or to make corn syrup and fuel. Their farms produce only corn, while a campesino's milpa provides corn, beans, squash, and other food.

Look for the bean plants, large squash leaves, and banana plant in this photo of a milpa. (See the picture of indigenous corn on page 75.)

Poisonous Products

Many chemical products used to increase crop production damage the environment, as well as farmworkers, wildlife, and people who eat the food. As people grow plants for fibers, food, medicines, and other uses, they may be harming the environment.

- **Rain runoff:** When it rains, water carries chemical fertilizers, pesticides, and herbicides used in farming into waterways and down to underground water aquifers (natural storage areas). This toxic runoff kills wetland animals and poisons well water. In California's San Joaquin Valley, considered the food basket of the world, the people who live in farming communities suffer from health problems caused by exposure to these poisons.

- **Bye-bye butterflies:** The increased use of herbicides (weed killers), particularly glyphosate in fields planted with GMO corn and other crops that are engineered to tolerate toxins, has had serious effects on people and wild animals. Herbicides kill all plants, except GMO crops, where they are sprayed. Thus weeds, as well as native wild plants, are killed. Caterpillars, such as those of the monarch butterfly, only eat certain plants. Monarchs are only found on milkweed. Herbicides have decimated milkweed and caused a major decline in the numbers of monarch butterflies. Since the 1990s, the number of monarch butterflies in North America has declined dramatically from over 700 million to a little more than 100 million.

- **Poison farms, poison food?** There is concern that some weed killers may cause health issues in humans. Despite the World Health Organization's claim that glyphosate does not cause cancer, some countries are starting to ban the product. In Argentina, there have been a large number of birth defects in communities near soybean farms with high weed killer use. Thousands of doctors in that country demanded that it be banned. Deaths linked to glyphosate in Sri Lanka resulted in the country banning its use. Another component, POEA, which helps glyphosate penetrate plant cells, may be the culprit in these health problems. In 2017, the state of California added glyphosate to its list of chemicals known to cause cancer.

- **Genetic pollution:** Botanists have traced the origin of the first corn crops to a wild grass that grows in the mountains of Mexico. In the remote mountain village of Capulalpam, descendants of the original farmers grow local varieties of corn passed down through generations. In 2001, two scientists discovered that genes from genetically modified corn had polluted the genes of native corn. Wild plants that crops have originated from are like a safety deposit box of genes. Many scientists now are worried that this gene pollution could erase the original genetic makeup of these original corn varieties that are the ancestors of all the current varieties of corn. These old varieties of corn are more likely to survive drastic changes in climate or new plant diseases. As the world's second most important food crop, this could have dire consequences.

Local Plant Citizens

Some plants, such as bracken fern, grow on every continent except Antarctica. Others, like red sandwort, grow all around the northern part of the world. Lyre leaf sage grows in 20 states. Southern river sage, however, is known only in Florida, where it grows in swamps. In an herb garden you may find *Salvia officinallis*, a sage native to southern Europe that is grown as a kitchen herb.

Saving Species from Extinction

Farming, logging, grazing, mining, and construction of roads, parking lots, and buildings create disturbances in natural landscapes. Plants that can easily grow in disturbed sites are known as pioneer species. Many pioneers become weeds in zones disturbed by people. Other pioneer species that can only grow after natural disturbances like wildfires or flood may become rare in the absence of these natural disturbances. Other plants become rare when their natural habitat is replaced with farms or rangeland, or when it's converted to suburbs or cities. Hundreds of plant species go extinct every decade in places like tropical rain forests as a result of logging and grazing. Some of these plants might have been helpful in treating a disease or might have had some other use as a raw material for human products. Some might have been the only source of food for a caterpillar or bee. Each species is special and its loss is irreversible. To many people each species is worth saving, just because, like us, it exists.

MEET YOUR SPECIAL PLANT NEIGHBORS

Research, plan, take a trip! No matter where you live, there is probably a nature refuge, park, botanic garden, or other protected natural area nearby. Even in New York City, the nation's most populous urban area, the Natural Areas Conservancy protects 20,000 acres of natural lands—including shorelines, forests, and wetlands—within the city boundaries. These are great places to get away from the hustle and bustle of daily life. Visit them to discover plants from your region or other parts of the planet.

MATERIALS

➤ Camera
➤ Plant journal
➤ Pen or pencil

1. Find out what kind of natural areas are near your home by asking people you know or by surfing the Internet. (Search the term *natural area* + the name of your town or city.)

2. Schedule a day and time with an adult family member or friend who can take you there.

3. Read about the area before you go to learn about special plants you can look for. For example, if you live in Chicago you might search for harebell or beach pea in one of the eight protected dune habitats within the city limits. See page 103 for help finding natural areas.

4. Be sure to bring a camera and your plant journal to record notes, take pictures, and sketch your discoveries.

Visit a botanic garden like this one to learn about the plants in your region.

Rescued from the Brink?

Five centuries after Europeans settled on Long Island, New York, it was hard to find native woodlands, meadows, and plains. Many plants and animal species had disappeared. With 7.5 million people living on the island, it would be a surprise if any species or plant communities unique to the region have survived. At one time there were over 60,000 acres of native bunchgrass prairies on Long Island. By the end of the 20th century there were barely 200 left.

These prairies once turned pink each spring with millions of sandplain gerardia (*Agalinis acuta*) blossoms. In 1987, when fewer than 1,000 plants existed, the species was designated as "critically imperiled" under the US Endangered Species Act.

Since then, by protecting the remaining prairie habitat on Long Island, and in Rhode Island, Massachusetts, Connecticut, and Maryland, the population grew to 80,000 by 2003. Fencing prairies to keep out the nonnative eastern cottontail, which devours sandplain gerardia, and igniting fires on the prairies to keep the grasslands shrub-free proved to be a lifesaver. As sandplain gerardia is the only endangered plant species in New York State, its recovery is especially symbolic.

Sandplain gerardia grows only in bunchgrass prairies.

Restoring Wild Lands

Preserving rare species and ecosystems requires restoring natural processes such as fire or flooding. In addition, special measures are necessary to protect, expand, and reestablish ecosystems such as sand prairies.

For thousands of years, Native Americans have used fire to maintain grasslands that special plants and animals depend on. Mowing or grass cutting favors the survival of grasses, such as little bluestem, the dominant bunchgrass in the sand plains. Grasses grow from their bases, whereas shrubs and nonnative invasive plants grow from stem tips. Carefully managed grazing by sheep or other livestock has the same results.

Special ecosystems like the sand plain grasslands are populated with plants adapted to their soil and water conditions. Long Island is a massive moraine, a deposit of glacial debris, with unique features such as outwash plains formed by fine sands inside the ice being deposited as the glacier melted. By restoring disturbed soils, biologists can provide the conditions for the grasses to thrive.

Whether in the high mountains, far north, or deserts, restoration biologists are

BE A PLANT PAL

Investigate, invigorate, instigate! Whether you live in the city or the country, there are plants that need your help. Even in Los Angeles, the second-largest city in the United States, there are natural areas with rare plants that need special care from volunteers. In Ballona Wetlands, not far from Los Angeles International Airport, one rare plant is thought to be extinct. But another species, the Ventura marsh milk vetch, may grow in the wetlands once again with the help of ecologists and volunteers. How can you help?

1. Find out about rare or threatened plants or plant communities in your area. There are probably organizations seeking volunteers to help protect these plants. Search for these organizations on the Internet and check to see if they need volunteers. If so, get an adult's permission to participate in workdays with your friends or family.

2. On your workday, take photos or video footage of the project.

3. Educate your classmates by sharing photos, video footage, and your personal experience working to protect the plants.

4. Start a campaign to have your school adopt a local rare or endangered plant.

5. Get other people to volunteer by inviting family, friends, or neighbors to a future restoration project.

exploring ways to aid threatened ecosystems along with the plants and animals that call them home.

Plant Workers

Many jobs require knowledge of plants. People in your community might be working with plants in jobs such as those in the following list. Perhaps you can chat with them or, better yet, shadow them for part of a workday. Ask your parents, guardian, or teacher to help you arrange this. What would you do as one of these plant workers?

- **Landscape architect:** Come up with the design of, for example, a park landscape, school campus, shopping center landscape, or private garden.

- **Nursery manager:** Oversee the planting and care of plants grown at a nursery and sold to gardeners or for planting in public spaces.

- **Yard and lawn care:** Be a combination doctor and barber for plants at a home garden, park, or university, or anywhere else where greenery needs attention.

- **Nature preserve manager:** Help natural processes in maintaining the health and diversity of native plant communities.

- **Botanist:** Monitoring, identifying, studying, and keeping records are some of the skills botanists use to help us understand the world of plants.

- **Seed supplier:** As the source of new plants, seeds need to be available to gardeners, farmers, and botanists restoring natural landscapes.

- **Restoration botanist:** Helping native plants reclaim human-altered areas requires the skills of a botanist, gardener, and landscape architect.

- **Herbalist:** Knowing which herbs to prescribe for ailments is an age-old skill. Homeopathic healers are trained at special schools. A license is required in some countries and some US states.

- **Florist:** People purchase flowers for weddings, funerals, and other special events from florists, who know which flowers are best for each particular situation.

- **Farmer or farmer's market vendor:** Fruit and vegetable farmers and gardeners make more money from their produce by selling directly to customers at farmer's markets. Many have yearlong customers who they supply weekly with a box or bag of produce. Called CSA (community supported agriculture), this arrangement provides customers with produce and the farmer with a steady income.

Moss of the World

One plant thrives on human and animal interference. No matter which continent you live on, you might step on a small reddish moss that is found throughout the globe. Redshank moss (*Ceratodon purpureus*) flourishes in disturbed areas, whether they are roadsides, cracks in sidewalks, parking lots, mine waste sites, or heavily trodden ground. In Antarctica, redshank moss colonizes soil left bare by melting glaciers or by wildlife disturbances. It is also called red roof moss for its habit of growing on shingles, or fire moss for its ability to colonize recently burned sites.

Redshank moss plants are either male or female, and both emit a special scent. Tiny springtail bugs prefer the female plants, and they improve fertilization of the moss. It is thought that they may be attracted to the scent in the same way that a bee is attracted to the scent of a flower. This may be one of the oldest mutually beneficial relationships of any plant and animal.

Redshank moss grows on every continent, as well as on islands in the South Pacific and Atlantic Oceans. Look for it in your neighborhood!

Plant Terms

annual: A plant that completes its life in one season

biennial: A plant that completes its life in two years

bud: A compact growth that develops into a flower, leaf, or new stem

cellulose: The main component of cell walls

cultivar: A variety of plant that has been created in cultivation through selective breeding

ecologist: A scientist who studies the interrelationships between plants, animals, and the environment

ecosystem: A system made up of plants, animals, and the landscape

exocarp: The outermost layer of a fruit

gene: A basic unit in an organism that carries traits from generation to generation

genus: Part of a plant or animal's scientific name (which is composed of a genus and species). For example the genus for a group of plants known as clovers is *Trifolium*. (In Latin *tri* means "three" and *folium* means "leaf.") All clovers have the same genus, but there are 300 species in the world.

GMO: A genetically modified organism that has had its genetic material altered by scientists

herbicide: A substance that kills plants

hormone: A substance transported in blood or sap that stimulates cells into action

hybrid: The offspring of two plants or animals of different species or varieties

lignin: A complex substance that adds rigidity to the cell walls of plants

mesocarp: The middle layer of a fruit

node: A slight swelling on a stem from which leaves or stems emerge

organism: An individual life form

ovary: A structure in which eggs develop

ovule: An egg

perennial: A plant that completes its life in three or more years

pericarp: The scientific term for a fruit

pesticide: A substance that kills insects and other invertebrates

phloem: The pipelike tissue in a plant through which sugars and other substances are transported from the leaves downward

photosynthesis: A process by which plants use sunlight to transform water and carbon dioxide into sugar and oxygen

pistil: The female part of a flower made up of the ovary, style, and stigma

radicle: The root that emerges from a seed

respiration: The process by which a plant uses oxygen to get energy from plant sugar, resulting in the release of carbon dioxide

rhizome: An underground stem that produces side shoots and roots

seed coat: The shield-like outer layer of a seed

sepal: A leaflike structure found below the other flower parts

species: Organisms so similar that they are able to reproduce together

spore: A tiny one-celled unit that can grow into a new organism

stamen: The male part of a flower made up of the filament and anthers

stolon: A creeping plant stem from which new plants sprout

transpiration: The process by which a plant takes in water through its roots, then expels water vapor from its leaves

tuber: A thickened underground stem that stores food and bears buds to produce new plants

vascular: Containing veins

vein: A tube that carries liquids

volatile: Easily vaporized at normal temperatures

wort: The Old English word for a plant with a medicinal or other use

xylem: The pipelike structure through which water and dissolved nutrients travel from the roots to all parts of a plant

Resources

There are many organizations, groups, and government agencies devoted to plants and conservation. Below are a few to get you started on your botanical journey.

American Horticultural Society: ahsgardening.org

American Public Gardens Association: https://publicgardens.org

Center for Invasive Species Management: www.weedcenter.org

National Audubon Society: www.audubon.org

National Park Service: www.nps.gov

Nature Conservancy: www.nature.org

North American Native Plant Society: www.nanps.org

Trust for Public Land: www.tpl.org

US Fish and Wildlife Service: www.fws.gov

US Forest Service: www.fs.fed.us

Teacher's Guide

The following are "plant prompts" for classroom activities or independent assignments.

1. Make a list of all the plants that students in the class know are growing in your community.

2. Conduct a survey of plants on the school grounds. Identify them with the help of a local expert (e.g., a landscaper, landscape architect, or nursery owner).

3. Connect math concepts students are learning with plant-related calculations or problem solving. For example, a weed such as a dandelion has pointed lobes. Students could figure out the average number of lobes per leaf.

4. Analyze a school lunch to determine the number of different plants it is made from.

5. Survey plants on the school grounds to find the largest and smallest ones.

6. Discuss community issues involving plants.

7. Look for plant stories in the news.

8. Have each student adopt a plant on the school grounds and learn as much as they can about it.

9. Make signs for plants on the school grounds with their names and an interesting fact.

10. Have students research plants in your region to discover if any plants are unique to your area.

11. Plan a class field trip to a nursery, nature preserve, or special garden.

12. Assemble an age-appropriate list of literature in which a plant or plants are an integral part of the story.

Selected Bibliography

* Denotes titles suitable for young readers.

Books

Anderson, Kat. *Tending the Wild*. Berkeley: University of California Press, 2013.

Baldwin, Bruce. *The Jepson Manual: Vascular Plants of California*. Berkeley: University of California Press, 2012.

Bonta, Marcia Meyers. *Women in the Field: America's Pioneering Women Naturalists*. College Station: Texas A&M Press, 1991.

Evans, Howard Ensign. *Life on a Little-Known Planet*. New York: E. P. Dutton, 1978.

Kimmerer, Robin Wall. *Braiding Sweetgrass*. Minneapolis: Milkweed Editions, 2013.

Murphy, Pat. *By Nature's Design*. San Francisco: Chronicle Books, 1993.

Olin, George. *House in the Sun: A Natural History of the Sonoran Desert*. Tucson, AZ: Western National Parks Association, 1994.

*Young, Paul. *The Botany Coloring Book*. Oakland, CA: Coloring Concepts, 1982.

Zomlefer, Wendy B. *Flowering Plant Families*. Chapel Hill: University of North Carolina Press, 1980.

Index

sweat bees, 66
sweetgrass, 93

T

tannins, 52, 91
taproots, 22
taste, of leaves, 43
terminal buds, 30, 31
texture, of leaves, 42
thallus, 8
thistle skeletons, *28, 51*
thrips, 70
tillers, *30*, 31
tomato hornworms, 50
toxic waste, 91–92
transpiration, 33
tread lightly (plant), 54
tubers
    root, 25
    stem, 38
tumbling flower beetles, 64

turmeric, 87
turnip roots, *22*

U

urushiol, 54
USS *Constitution*, 88
utricles, 74

V

vascular plants, 9, 10, 28
veins, 4, 28, 38, 44, *44, 51*
vines, 10
violets, *63*, 65

W

wastewater treatment, 92
water management
    and leaf structure, 9, 49, 50
    and stems, 31, 33

watermeal, 3
watermelons, 74, 81
wax, on leaves, 49
weed killers, dangers of,
    94–95
weevils, 18
wort, 8

X

xylem, 31, 33

Y

yarrow, 87
yucca moths, 68, *68*, 70
yucca plants, 42, *42*

Z

zucchini squashes, *74*